Blessings by the Handful

A woman's celebration of faith and family

Rachel Tacke

NORTHWESTERN PUBLISHING HOUSE
Milwaukee, Wisconsin

Library of Congress Control Number: 2002114460
Northwestern Publishing House
1250 N. 113th St., Milwaukee, WI 53226-3284
© 2003 Northwestern Publishing House
www.nph.net
Published 2003
Printed in the United States of America
ISBN 0-8100-1516-1

To my best friend,

my encourager,

my lifetime companion,

my dear husband, Mark

Contents

Editor's Preface

For Martin Luther the female perspective was deserving of great admiration. "Earth has nothing more tender," he wrote, "than a woman's heart when it is the abode of piety."

How remarkably true and wise! Women perceive life in a way that is profoundly different from a man's understanding. Sometimes the differences are subtle. At other times a woman's viewpoint stands in bold juxtaposition to a male's view. Subtle or stark, a woman's view on life is inevitably unique because it uses the human heart as its filter.

This book is part of an effort to give voice to the expressions of godly women in every walk and stage of life. The purpose of this book and others like it is to examine the great themes and important struggles that are part of every Christian woman's experience—to help her explore her blessings, examine her faith, inspire her family, endure her suffering, excel in her prayer life, and become fully engaged in the worship of her Savior-God.

In a world gone giddy with the ideology of radical feminism, these books written by women and for women provide a meaningful dialogue bathed in the light of God's eternal Word. May the give and take of these timeless conversations bring glory to God's holy name and a rich harvest of blessings to this book's reader.

Kenneth J. Kremer, editor

Introduction

My life is not my own. And that is the greatest blessing. Life is an unending miracle. It grows—constantly changing, expanding, returning to itself. My faith, a complete gift, directs me to the keeper of my life. Faith gives me eyes to see God's care in my daily life. Faith gives me understanding as I search Scripture to learn more about this gift of life. And it is my faith that shows the need to celebrate, to express joy and thanks to my God.

This book is about the moments of change that life brings. Sometimes they come unexpectedly, bringing joy. But often change can be difficult.

The Bible teaches me through these moments of change. Written so long ago, it speaks eloquently today, because there is nothing new under the sun. The ancient characters are my brothers and sisters in Christ. Their experiences reveal how God guided them and blessed them, keeping all the promises he made to them. God does the same for me. As I experience his hand in my life, I see the many blessings he gives. The Bible does not hem me in as a woman. Instead, it defines me as a child of God. It guides me. The Bible shows how salvation frees me for a life of service. This is the key to contentment.

It is my hope that what follows will offer insights and help to others in times of change. Then, with a life of service, they too can bear witness to the blessings that God gives—blessings by the handful.

CHAPTER ONE

Captive in Conversation

She sprawled across my bed, interrupting my reading. Her long brown hair framed her face. The afternoon sun stretched its long fingers across the quilt with inviting warmth. She moved closer for a hug.

"Some of my friends want to grow up to look like the women in magazines. They want to have jobs that make lots of money. They want to wear fancy clothes and be glamorous. But I don't want that . . . I want to be just like you." There was a thoughtful pause, then, "Mom, why are you so cuddly?" The question didn't need an answer, but it unlocked a flow of thoughts waiting to come pouring out.

Enough silence followed for my mind to catch the "not beautiful" innuendo. Putting my book aside, I gave her a questioning glance.

"No, Mom," she continued, "I didn't mean that. It's just that you're so . . . comfortable. You're beautiful without all those things, and I want to be just like you."

Now she had my attention. Our daughter has a gift for bringing joy to those around her. The words from a proverb echoed in my mind: May she who gave you birth rejoice!

Smiling, I soaked up the affection and hugged her. The afternoon sun felt warm and inviting. Instinctively I knew that this was going to be a special *mother-daughter moment*—in other words, a long conversation.

Our youngest child enjoys talking, especially when there are no interruptions, such as siblings competing for my attention.

Now she had me all to herself. "You know what, Mom? I'm going to have lots of children." The authority of her statement demanded acceptance.

Glancing into my future, I smiled. "Good! That way I can spoil them."

She turned slowly, satisfied that I had approved her plan. My desire to read dissolved as I looked into her big, luminous eyes. Those eyes! I remember her intense stare as a newborn. Her serious, searching dark eyes never left my face.

Life—what a precious gift!

"Wait a minute." My voice interrupted the silence. "I thought you were never going to have any children. That's what you said in kindergarten." Katherine laughed, remembering. It had been during one of those many trips home after school. That time the kindergarten carpool discussion was about future plans. Her best friend, who planned to be a vet, explained to Katherine how babies are born. No, not how they are made, just born. My daughter's shocked response was "Well, then I'm certainly not going to have any!"

A serious conversation between the two kindergartners followed. The next question was directed to me: "Mom, when you grow up, do you have to get married?" Of course, she knew that married people have babies. By the end of the trip, the backseat committee had decided they were going to own a farm with two houses and two barns. The barns would hold chickens, cows, and horses. The houses would contain an assortment of pets and two husbands . . . just to do all the farm chores.

In the warmth of this afternoon's sunshine, an older, wiser Katherine reassured me: "Don't worry, Mom. I don't think that way anymore." Again she paused. "But maybe I'll still live on a farm." Her future plans were changing as quickly as the size of her tennis shoes. Another gentle hug and a warm silence followed. And then, "Were you scared to have babies? I mean, what was it like? What did I do?"

We talked about how wonderfully God's design works. And once again I thanked God for putting this wonderful person in my life, embracing the reality of Psalm 37: "Delight yourself in the LORD and he will give you the desires of your heart."

Life—what a privilege!

The plan: God's . . . and mine

Looking at our long, gangly daughter, I reminisced about how my life has changed. Plans before marriage had been so simple: move into a nice little house, work for awhile, and then, fill the house with four, five, or maybe even six children. After Mark graduated from college, we would settle where our teaching careers took us. We were young, in love, and eager to begin our lives together.

But God's thoughts were not as simple as our thoughts. He designed a more complex and beautiful plan.

The first year of marriage passed, then the second. Work filled our days, but each night we returned to a quiet, empty house with no children.

As the years passed, our hopes were stifled. Dissatisfaction, discontent, and eventually a silent despair began to creep into the events of every day. The doctors were unable to reassure us; test results were meaningless. Our prayers seemed to go unanswered. Stress and anxiety intruded into my work, my home, my marriage. I was blind to the possibility that God was using this time to strengthen my faith with patience and maturity. I could not see his love being poured out daily. I could not imagine the blessings that awaited me—blessings beyond measure and so rich with his goodness that I would never be able to fully grasp or appreciate—blessings far beyond the handful that a child would have meant for me at that time. The beauty in my daily surroundings had all but vanished. It was time to learn how to trust God's wisdom for my life.

Even though God knew the desire of my heart from the very beginning, his plan unfolded slowly. It would take time for me to grasp the words of the psalmist: "I trust in the LORD. I will be glad and rejoice in your love, for you saw my affliction and knew the anguish of my soul" (Psalm 31:6,7).

At times in my life when I do not understand, I turn to the Bible for answers. There I search for examples to guide me in my day-to-day living. In times of joy I find words of praise; in times of weakness, strength; in my muddled confusion, direction. God's Word fills my needs—always. His Word renews my life with hope and beauty. As I read about his people of long ago, I learn about myself—my struggles, my wrestling with him, my dreams, my faith. Their lives teach me, challenge me, and encourage me.

Abram and Sarai

The Genesis account of Sarai and Abram has long held my attention. Imagine yourself in the sandals of Sarai or Abram. Young love. A promising career. The excitement of beginning a new life in a new place. But, most of all, the Lord himself promising to guide, to bless, and to make his name great through your offspring.

Sarai had her blessings too. I do understand that people lived longer in those days, but imagine being as beautiful as Sarai and capturing the attention of a king at the age of 65!

Yet, with all of this wealth, beauty, and success, there was no baby for Sarai and Abram. No tiny infant to hold in their arms. No new life from their shared love. How this must have weighed on their hearts!

Time passed. Abram brought his plans concerning his inheritance before the Lord: "You have given me no children; so a servant in my household will be my heir."

With great patience and gentleness the Lord took Abram outside. A visual lesson was needed. "Look up at the heavens and count the stars—if indeed you can count them," God said to Abram. "So shall your offspring be."

I remember one clear night as a child, camping under the stars. The desert stillness hurt my ears. There were no tall trees. No uneven skyline hampered my field of vision. And the stars were brilliant in the distance; it was like looking into forever. I have always imagined that it was the kind of sky Abram saw. I could also imagine Abram with Sarai, gazing at those stars, dreaming of their future, believing God's promises.

Years passed.

Years: the blink of an eye to our timeless, eternal God. The years passed in my own life. There were not six kids, not four either, just an empty house with two cats in the yard, a dog, and a loving husband. With such narrow vision, it was as though I were walking through a beautiful garden, seeing only the occasional stray weed.

Unfair! That's the word I thrust at God. "Here I am, Lord, doing your will. I've given my life, my time, to your service. I've been honest with my words, faithful in my marriage. How come I'm not getting what I want?" I became focused on myself and saw only failure in my life. A dark shroud of self-directed thoughts and bruised emotions covered me.

Genesis chapter 16 talks about Ishmael, Abram's baby boy born by his Egyptian maidservant. This was done at Sarai's urging and certainly not in keeping with God's plan. But Abram was 86 years old. Along with time come second thoughts, angry challenges, self-doubt.

When Abram was 99, God came and renewed his covenant: "Your name will be Abraham, for I have made you a father of many nations. . . . As for Sarai . . . her name will be Sarah. I will bless her and will surely give you a son by her. I will bless her so that she will be the mother of nations; kings of peoples will come from her."

When Abraham looked up at that night sky, he was reminded of his descendants—all those whose lives were planned by God before time started ticking. My husband (the stargazer), my neighbors, my parents and grandparents, Sunday school teachers and students, as well as the prophet Samuel, King David, and Saint Paul. It boggles the logical mind. Each person fits into this plan, woven in at the exact time and place God has chosen. How perfectly intricate! How vast are his plans! How elegant and dynamic! Since he brought Eve to Adam, his plan was for conception through love within the beautiful nest of marriage. In hindsight I can now appreciate what Saint Paul had in mind long ago when he wrote, "Oh, the depth of the riches of the wisdom and knowledge of God! How unsearchable his judgments and his paths beyond tracing out!" (Romans 11:33).

How much I learned from Abraham and Sarah! My first encounters with Abraham and Sarah go back to early childhood. I pictured Sarah making that meal for those heavenly guests in Genesis chapter 18. I envisioned her peeking through the tent opening as she laughed inwardly. But, at that young age, I could not imagine the profound joy she must have experienced when she realized that she was pregnant. Later I could understand. And of Abraham's unwavering faith! The Bible says: "Without weakening in his faith, he faced the fact that his body was as good as dead—since he was about a hundred years old—and that Sarah's womb was also dead. Yet he did not waver through unbelief regarding the promise of God, but was strengthened in his faith and gave glory to God, being fully persuaded that God had power to do what he had promised. This is why 'it was credited to him as righteousness'" (Romans 4:19-22).

A season of hope

As the years passed, so did the obsession with filling our home with children. Plans for the future changed. I focused on simply serving the Lord in the present.

Then, in his own time, the Lord answered our prayers. He blessed us with three children: Dan, Elizabeth, and Katherine—each a unique and wonderful person—a soul to cherish.

Like Sarah, I had doubted, planned my own strategies, focused on myself, laughed at inappropriate times, made mistakes. Sin was always creeping around my door. Then I found comfort in reading about Abraham and Sarah. I was reminded how God took care of them. How they prayed and waited. How they sinned and were forgiven. How God's plan of salvation covers all weaknesses, even doubt. Their story gave me hope when I needed it most.

My prayers and my focus changed. God had given me a new perspective. With the writer of Psalm 30, I could now sing: "You turned my wailing into dancing; you removed my sackcloth and clothed me with joy, that my heart may sing to you and not be silent. O LORD my God, I will give you thanks forever."

The new life brought to Sarah and Abraham was the fulfillment of the Lord's promise. Sarah's joy was complete. She sang, "God has brought me laughter, and everyone who hears about this will laugh with me."

In her old age Sarah nurtured little Isaac. He grew, played, laughed, cried—a precious gift from God. Abraham must have spent time with young Isaac, pointing up at the stars in the dead of night, telling Isaac of the heavenly Father's promises. And then together they would smile.

Psalm 8 says it so well: "O LORD, our Lord, how majestic is your name in all the earth! You have set your glory above the heavens. From the lips of children and infants you have ordained praise."

Celebrate life!

I looked again at our beautiful daughter Katherine. Her long, slender arms encircled my waist. I treasured her, everything about her, from her big feet to her infectious laugh.

"Mom," she asks, "is it okay if I stay awhile and read with you?"

Smiling with satisfaction, I open my Bible and together we contemplate the beautiful words of Psalm 139: "O LORD, you have searched me and you know me. You know when I sit and when I rise; you perceive my thoughts from afar. You discern my going out and my lying down; you are familiar with all my ways."

CHAPTER TWO

Present Insanity

It was one of those *long* days. The family schedule had been carefully planned, but something was wrong. A gloomy bank of clouds hung heavy with anticipation, setting an ominous mood as I drove to pick up our daughter. A nagging little voice kept saying, "You're forgetting something." I racked my brain. I am one of those people who can never remember where I last set my coffee cup. As I waited for another red light to change, I checked the calendar in my purse. It agreed with the master schedule posted on the fridge door. Apparently there was nothing to worry about; I was still in control. The day included school, music lessons, catechism class, a basketball game, and an evening meeting. Sandwiched in between, our family would sit down together for supper. If the traffic co-operated, everything should fit together like a giant jigsaw puzzle. So why the nagging voice?

As I pulled into the church parking lot to drop Elizabeth off for catechism class, that nagging feeling gave way to reality. Our teenage son had stayed after school for a basketball game. And he had the house key! He had not gone home with Katherine in the carpool. That meant our seven-year-old daughter would be dropped off at a locked, empty house . . . alone. There was a moment of panic, some anger, then mostly frustration. The ugly, gray clouds emptied themselves in a downpour.

The traffic was uncooperative and I crawled home. Every light glared red, taunting me. I had plenty of time to focus on my frustrations. With a torrent of questions, my mood turned as ugly as the dark, wet sky. Why me? What happened to my control? Wasn't I supposed to be the organized one? I have my own work to do too, places to go, people to meet, a life to live. What had happened to my unfettered goals for family simplicity? Why was I always the one driving? And, most important, where was my daughter?

As I pulled into my driveway, I tried to calm myself. A quick search showed that Katherine was not waiting at home alone by a locked door. I walked across the street, systematically eliminating the possibilities. Thank God that Kara, my neighbor, was there.

Knocking on the door, I asked, "Is she here?" When I heard Katherine's voice coming up from downstairs, I felt a quick flood of relief and my heart stopped pounding.

We walked across the street, and I took Katherine's hand and fumbled for the right words to apologize for not being home. She pulled away. "Mom!" she said angrily. "Where were you? Why wasn't anyone home? Why was the house locked? I thought something happened to you!"

I took my daughter in my arms, and we talked. My explanations didn't excuse what had happened, but the hug soothed both of us, and we continued on with our day.

Later I thought about the incident. Why had I become so anxious, so angry? And how had life gotten so out of control?

With supper simmering I retraced my route, driving back to retrieve the rest of my family from church and school. Katherine, happily chattering in the front seat beside me, had graciously forgiven and even forgotten the trauma. The red lights were still gleefully exerting their power over traffic. My eyes were drawn to the faces of others driving past. Empty faces—all chasing their own thoughts, their own paths. And I was one of them, another empty face. Except I had a chattering seat-belted child beside me.

I smiled at Katherine, encouraging more conversation. It was then that the little voice returned, not in a nagging tone this time, but quietly echoing some familiar words from Ecclesiastes. "When I surveyed all that my hands had done and what

I had toiled to achieve, everything was meaningless, a chasing after the wind; nothing was gained under the sun."

I picked up my family members, and we returned home to a warmed-up supper. Chores got done. The rest of the day fit together perfectly, like a giant jigsaw puzzle. But as my head hit the pillow, I confessed the sins of being too focused on myself, and I prayed for guidance.

Organizing life by lists

When I was a teen, I was sure certain things wouldn't happen to me. I had started a list: "Things I won't do when I'm a grown-up." I had lots of items on this list; such as, "When I am a parent I will never say *Because I said so.*" My list was full of points to make my life better.

As I grew older, the items on the list began to change into "Things I *want in life.*" I wanted a lot too. Nothing too extravagant—a handsome husband, a good job where I could use my talents, a loving family, a beautiful home. It sounded very nice. I loved dreaming.

Later my list changed once again as my goals became clearer. The items on the list were more refined and sophisticated now, and the header read something like "Things *that are important* in life." Not only did I want a handsome husband, but he had to be just the right one. My list was carefully subdivided into subheads that included a specific, point-by-point description of this dream spouse. Then I prayed about it: *Dear Lord, help me find someone who cares about you more than the things in this world. I need someone who is like-minded. Someone who doesn't love money or the things money can buy. But, instead, someone who loves the simple things in life, someone who finds joy in your creation. Someone who has a gentle spirit and is loving and caring.*

I prayed a lot about this list. For me it was all or nothing.

Eliezer's task

There is a wonderful example of this in the life of Abraham. Sarah had died. Genesis chapter 24 tells us that "Abraham was now old and well advanced in years, and the LORD had blessed him in every way." But Abraham wanted one more thing—a good wife for his son, Isaac. She couldn't be just any woman either. She had to be from Abraham's kin, and she should believe in the true God. There was only one small problem. Abraham's kin lived halfway across the continent.

The Bible recounts the journey of Eliezer, the chief servant of Abraham's household, as he traveled to Mesopotamia. His mission was to find the right woman for Isaac. Then he was to convince her to travel with him back to Canaan. There she was to marry someone she had never met. Eliezer also had to convince the parents of the intended bride to let her go. They would probably never see their daughter again. Though it was the custom for parents to arrange the marriages of their children, they could never hope to meet their daughter's husband—their son-in-law, Isaac.

Abraham made Eliezer swear that he would bring a wife back for Isaac, and Eliezer took his oath seriously. Isaac was the son born to Abraham and Sarah later in life when they thought bearing children was impossible. Once, in obedience to God's command, Abraham had been willing to offer Isaac as a sacrifice. This wife for Isaac had to also please the Lord God, whose every word Eliezer's master obeyed. God had said in his covenant-promise with Abraham, "To your offspring I will give this land." In the light of that promise, Eliezer's task was hardly a trivial matter. And Abraham did not let Eliezer go empty handed. "The LORD, the God of heaven, who brought me out of my father's household and my native land . . . he will send his angel before you so that you can get a wife for my son from there." Eliezer relied on these words of blessing and promise.

When Eliezer arrived in the faraway town, the very first thing he did was to say a prayer. "Before he had finished praying, Rebekah came out with her jar on her shoulder." The beautiful account of the union between Isaac and Rebekah, as planned by God himself, unfolds in the rest of the chapter. The Bible adds: "The girl was very beautiful, a virgin; no man had ever lain with her." And the happy ending? "Isaac brought her into the tent of his mother Sarah, and he married Rebekah. So she became his wife, and he loved her."

The Lord knows our needs. He wants what is good for us. And when we pray, he not only hears, he answers. And sometimes he answers in such spectacular fashion that, if we aren't paying attention, we altogether fail to see them as his blessings.

This almost happened in my case. My own prayers were answered. But I didn't realize at first that this had happened. Then one day in my college dorm room, I found that old piece of paper with my prayer still scribbled on it. I read once again what I had asked for. Every detail listed in the heads and subheads on that piece of paper had been answered without my being aware of it. I did not show my best friend that piece of paper until years later. I had it all—my husband, my best friend, my companion in life. We appreciated the same things in life, laughed together, planned together, prayed together, worshiped together. And I had also been blessed with the family, the home, and the job where I could use my talents serving the Lord. I was blessed beyond the boundaries of my own dreams. With David, I could say, "You have made known to me the path of life; you will fill me with joy in your presence, with eternal pleasures at your right hand" (Psalm 16:11).

More lists

But my list making didn't stop. By observing other Christian families, I realized that there was more that I wanted. I took note of the family with four young children who could sit up front in church without bribes or toys. I wanted that! The family that sits together, prays together, worships together. I also observed families in which older children returned to the homes of their childhood with children of their own. The grandparents were so proud, walking their grandchildren by the hand into the pew. I wanted that too.

I studied the families of the young children who were students in my classroom. Some were happy and secure, unhindered in their learning, willing to give and take. They stood in stark contrast with others. I wondered why. Many of the homes of those students with a healthy outlook did not stress the *creed of more:* more house, more clothes, more toys, more success, more sports, more friends, more power, more money, and so on. The kids who were truly happy, secure, and respectful students came from happy, secure, respectful homes. As children, they were read to, hugged often, fed well, put to bed on time. They were guided and disciplined too. Their parents took time for their children. Someone was at home, greeting children when they came home after school. Parents were there, actively involved in their lives when their children needed them. Love was given and received. And they worshiped together, putting the Lord first in their lives. I wanted all of that for our children. I wanted to read to our children, sing with them, go on long exploring walks with them, cook and clean for them. I wanted my family to have a high priority in my life.

The Lord blessed our marriage with children. Oh, the excitement! The awe! The fatigue! I had thought I knew for sure what I wanted in life, but I didn't even know how to pin a diaper. And those times in church! "Training up our children" sometimes took so much effort that we completely missed hearing the sermon. (Once, when the offering plate was passed, Katherine opened her mouth and let a quarter roll out down her tongue. Plunk! It made an odd, wet sound when it landed among the other offerings.)

Life has not been in my control for a long time. So, when those long days come, and I ask "How did I get stuck in this moment?" I will be able to refocus, and maybe the list will need to be rewritten. As of this moment, this is the list of what I pray for:

THINGS THAT ARE TRULY MEANINGFUL

I pray that . . .
    my family will grow in God's grace, living life according
    to his Word, worshiping and praying together.

we will use our time, talents, and blessings to serve the
Lord and his church.
my children will keep the Lord close to their hearts, using
his guidance in their future decisions and plans.
my family will work together, and that my children
will appreciate the value of hard work and the
satisfaction it brings.
we will also play together, laugh together, and enjoy
being together.
my children will grow up being respectful, thankful, and
caring.
my children will learn to love learning.
my family will live in an environment filled with love
and contentment.

Meaningless? Hardly. A chasing after the wind? Not when it is centered on Christ. But there are still times when I lose my focus. Making beds, cleaning rooms, folding laundry could, I suppose, in a certain way be categorized as meaningless. Like the sun that rises, sets, and hurries back to where it rises, or the wind that blows to the south and turns to the north, round and round it goes, ever returning on its course. There will always be dishes to wash and that never-ending pile of laundry. Beds will always need making. In spite of those things, there is still meaning to be found in the Christian home.

So what will I say the next time that nagging little voice comes to haunt me? Well, it helps keep me focused. It steers me back to God. And for that I am grateful. But, for finding meaning in the life God has given me, the words of Ecclesiastes chapter 3 seem to fit best: "I know that there is nothing better for [me] than to be happy and do good while [I] live. That everyone may eat and drink, and find satisfaction in all his toil—this is the gift of God." And I will continue to pray for the things that are truly meaningful—and especially for guidance and wisdom. We have entered the uncharted waters of the dreaded years of parenting teenagers. How we need guidance and wisdom! But I know just where to get it. "All

Scripture is God-breathed and is useful for teaching, rebuking, correcting and training in righteousness, so that the man of God may be thoroughly equipped for every good work" (2 Timothy 3:16,17). Ah, a new thing for the current list: *that my teens will be thoroughly equipped for doing good.*

Some people chase after the wind; I will keep on chasing after the schedule on the refrigerator door. Sometime, when you get stuck at a red light, look around at all the empty faces. Maybe you'll see me there. I'll be the one smiling.

CHAPTER THREE

Stitches from the Past

The heat of a summer day was just beginning to gather. I was on a mission. Elizabeth's second birthday was approaching. I wanted something very special for this momentous occasion. Something that would go with Elizabeth through the years. Something of value.

The idea had crept out slowly, like a timid puppy, wagging its tail, waiting for acceptance. As it took shape my excitement grew. Now, driving along the road to an old farmhouse, my joy bubbled over with anticipation.

The gift would be a quilt. Not just any quilt. A quilt hand stitched by my dear Aunt Gertrude. That would be Elizabeth's cherished birthday present—a present from the past.

The dust along the Minnesota back road rose in the heat. It settled with the sounds of the meadowlarks and crickets from the low growth along the ditches. A familiar bank of trees guided me through the last turn. Endless fields stretched before me in every direction, green with new growth. Peonies, still heavy with the weight of morning dew, bowed low along the gravel driveway. I passed the kitchen garden, past the swing by the shade tree, and came to a stop next to a stately, white house. I shut the motor off and sat in the warm stillness, soaking in every part of this special day for a daughter who was still too young to remember.

The familiar slam of the screen door on the front porch interrupted my reverie. I looked up to see Aunt Gertrude's welcome smile and open arms. The hug that followed felt wonderful. It was not unexpected. We chatted as she motioned me toward the front steps.

The house was as inviting as ever. Farm cats peered from their hiding places, then scampered down the path where my car had just brought billows of dust up from the dry roadbed. We walked up the steps, into the cool shade of the porch. It was just as it had been in my childhood—comfortable wicker chairs covered with afghans, a toy box still full of antique farm toys, a cot waiting for a summer afternoon's nap. Plants filled the windowsills, gathering their strength. In the corner was Aunt Gertrude's quilting basket.

We walked into the kitchen where my aunt had fixed a snack. I was directed to a chair that shone spotless, like the rest of the kitchen. I set Elizabeth in the wooden highchair, still sturdy through many years of use. The napkin holder on the table held a devotion book and a well-worn Bible.

I helped my daughter fold her hands as we gave thanks for our food. A picture of an old gentleman thanking God for his food hung on the wall behind her. It seemed to reflect the table before me: freshly baked bread, a plate of sausage slices and cheese, and familiar jars containing pickles and jam. My aunt said that she was sorry this was all she had to offer. I didn't object. No words could explain what a priceless feast it was.

Aunt Gertrude and Uncle Hans had lived in that white farmhouse forever. They worked their days farming, helping others, and serving God. Their little country church was a short distance down the dusty road. They had no children of their own, but the many blessings showered on them from the Lord overflowed to all who came under their roof.

We talked. I brought Aunt Gertrude up to date on my family. Elizabeth's constant chattering teased the joy lines in my aunt's noble face.

After lunch I put Elizabeth down for a nap on the same cot where I had taken naps as a child. Then Aunt Gertrude and I climbed the worn stairs to the second-floor bedroom where she stored her quilts. Dust floated gracefully in streams of sunshine that poured through the ancient window glass. As she opened an old, wooden chest, the scent of cedar spilled into the room. There lay the quilts of delicate stitches, dancing across a kaleidoscope of colors and patterns—each geometric shape fixed to its neighbor by small, perfect threads that had no beginning and no end.

Tenderly, Aunt Gertrude unfolded each quilt, one by one. The sunshine, streaming across the colors, accentuated their brightness. Years of patient labor were laid out before us until emotions overwhelmed me and tears of appreciation filled my eyes. These were priceless—labors of relentlessly patient love.

"This was Hans' shirt," she said, pointing to an olive-colored patch with a small print. I realized these quilts were her way of sharing pockets of her life with others, even after she would no longer be around to tell the stories that matched the cloth patches. "And here's a dress I made the Easter that your family moved." I tried to envision the outfit that she could see clearly. I knew so little of this woman, my mother's sister.

A slam of the screen door announced that Uncle Hans was home. "This one is yours," she said, handing me a beautiful garden basket quilt. It shimmered with delicate pastels that cascaded out of a blue and white background.

Together we carefully refolded the other quilts and restored them to their appointed places, nestling them between folds of tissue paper. Then we left the room's wooden floor, dancing rays of dusty light, and the pastiche of colors to their quiet, undisturbed rest.

We met Uncle Hans in the sitting room, where Aunt Gertrude served glasses of cold lemonade. "Let me show you what I'm working on," she said, pulling out perfect hexagons in various colors and patterns. Her aged hands suddenly took on the free movement of familiarity as she demonstrated the ancient mysteries of even seams and smooth corners. In seconds her deft fingers had composed another masterpiece of color and harmony, adding to the work in her hands. What a remarkably gentle and patient woman sat before me, wise beyond my years! And I yearned for the everyday work of the farm, the garden, the laying up food for the winter. These seemed to be luxuries from the past—the contentment of busy hands, food flavored with the taste of "just picked" or "freshly baked," conversations in the cool evening hours, and deep, refreshing sleep after a fulfilling day.

Elizabeth woke from her nap. Her hair was wet and curly from the dampness of her sleep. She took many sips of cool lemonade, brushing the frosty glass against her rosy cheeks. I wanted to stay—to absorb more of this place, but it was time to go. Another town in another state and another kind of life demanded my attention.

I gathered my precious belongings: a warm loaf of bread, a pint of Aunt Gertrude's deep-green rind pickles, the quilt, and my daughter. We hugged each other again—a concentrated hug—and wished one another *God's blessings.* Then off Elizabeth and I went, bumping down the driveway, past the limp peonies and playful cats. My aunt and uncle stood side by side, waving until the bend in the road removed them from my sight.

Tears wet my cheeks once more as the dust rose in clouds behind us. From her car seat Elizabeth peered at me in studied confusion. "Mama?"

A noble woman

In today's world my place as a woman can be confusing. Women are struggling to find their identities. "Your self-worth is measured by your accomplishments." "Find out who you are." "You owe it to yourself." Mixed messages, all of them. And they are proclaimed and promoted by virtually every medium. As some women climb up the ladder of prestige and success, others climb down in pursuit of simpler, more meaningful lives.

We have forgotten to look to the aging women around us with respect for their wisdom. Time and distance often remove us from these intimate relationships from which we can glean the experiences of lives lived to God's glory.

Proverbs chapter 31 and 1 Timothy offer two interesting and, in some ways, contrasting (but not contradictory) views of godly womanhood. Proverbs speaks of a woman strong for her tasks:

> A wife of noble character who can find? She is worth far more than rubies. Her husband has full confidence in her and lacks nothing of value. She brings him good, not harm, all the days of her life. . . . She sees that her trading is profitable. . . . She opens her arms to the poor. . . . She makes coverings . . . linen garments. She is clothed with strength and dignity; she can laugh at the days to come. She speaks with wisdom, and faithful instruction is on her tongue. She watches over the affairs of her household and does not eat the bread of idleness. . . . Charm is deceptive, and beauty is fleeting; but a woman who fears the LORD is to be praised.

At the same time, 1 Timothy teaches, "A woman should learn in quietness and full submission." These two portions of Scripture portray very different images: one strong; the other, by worldly standards at least, weak. My Aunt Gertrude had strength, dignity, and wisdom. She was forceful when tasks demanded it. Yet her strength had its quiet side as well. And her life demonstrated that wisdom can be submissive.

The world with its confusion is out there reaching for my daughters. In my own efforts at parenting, I have taught them to question things, so I wonder if they will see the strength in a quiet and willing spirit. I wonder too if they will be able to grasp the wisdom of being submissive or understand the joys that are to be found in a life of service.

When I look at my aunt, I also see my grandmother and my mom, as well as myself. We all have the same determined set to our jaws, the same twinkling eyes when we laugh. I am frequently recognized as my mother's daughter. My daughters have some of the same features, though their personalities are quite unique.

There is something else passed down from one generation to the next. I grew up in a family where devotions followed every evening meal. Saturdays were days of work. Saturday night baths, clean clothes laid out, a good night's sleep were all preparations for Sunday. The whole schedule revolved around our Sunday worship in God's house. There was never a question about going to church. We worshiped as a family. Then we ate Sunday dinner as a family and relaxed in the afternoon and evening together as a family.

When we went to bed at night, we prayed. My mother often sang a song she had learned as a child, "*Müde bin ich, geh' zur Ruh'.*" Now she sings the same wonderful tune to her grandchildren each time we're together as she nestles them in her arms.

Now the light has gone away;
Father, listen while I pray,
Asking you to watch and keep
And to send me quiet sleep.

I like to express things in my life through the tip of a paintbrush, dipping the rich, soft bristles into the delicate colors, softened with water. A stark white piece of paper is transformed by the cool, wet colors as they play with the light. I try to capture what holds beauty and meaning in my life. The quilt made by my Aunt Gertrude has appeared in several of my paintings. But my favorite is the painting of two-year-old Elizabeth, kneeling by her small bed, praying. Her soft curls fall gently around her face as she looks up. The title is *Now the Light Has Gone Away.*

Beautiful submission

Strength. Dignity. Beauty. Submission. They aren't so much taught as they are lived.

In all my years growing up, I never saw submission as something negative. It was a beautiful blend in marriage. I saw the words of Ephesians chapter 5 lived in easy times and in difficult times. "Wives, submit to your husbands as to the Lord. . . . Husbands, love your wives, just as Christ loved the church and gave himself up for her." Submission has never slowed me down in my service to the Lord. Instead, I have always found my life brimming with possibilities and overflowing with opportunities to serve.

Strength, quiet dignity, tender beauty, and certainly submission can all be seen in Jesus' life. To the raging storm, he simply said, "Quiet!" When a mob of angry accusers was ready to stone a sinful woman, he calmly knelt down and wrote in the sand with his finger. He gathered young children to himself when others thought he was too tired to be disturbed. And it was Jesus who knelt down to scrub the dirt off his disciples' feet. There is great wisdom in looking to Jesus not only as our Savior, but also as a perfect example of the kind of qualities Christian women are seeking.

The words Jesus used to calm the stormy Sea of Galilee may not have much effect on the the storms that sometimes rage between our teenagers. A simple *Quiet!* just doesn't do it. Neither does *Because I said so.* I point them to the Scriptures instead.

Our children know Jesus intimately. Their love for their Savior can also guide them to "Be imitators of God, therefore, as dearly loved children and live a life of love, just as Christ loved us and gave himself up for us as a fragrant offering and sacrifice to God" (Ephesians 5:1,2). Just as I continue to learn and grow in faith, so do my children. As I was taught, they are being taught. Their faith is being strengthened daily through regular contact with God's Word. And then his truth is applied daily in their young lives. The cycle never ends: he forgives, then we live for him by following his example.

Jesus, Savior, wash away
All that has been wrong today.
Help me ev'ry day to be
Good and gentle, more like Thee.

Our daughters never really got to know my Aunt Gertrude. They have only vague memories of a farm, some playful cats, and a stately, old, white house. But the quilt remains—a reminder of the many expressions of Christian womanhood.

CHAPTER FOUR

New Beginnings

In the summer after graduation from college, my husband and I moved to Michigan. He was to be the new principal of a small Christian elementary school and was scheduled to teach grades 6 through 8. My degree was also in education, but his school was already fully staffed, so I was resigned to the prospect of not teaching that year. Then came a phone call. A large school in a small neighboring town, 30 miles away, needed someone to teach departmentalized science in the upper grades. We established our first credit, to buy another car, and I threw myself into my new job.

The first day of that school year lingers vividly in my memory. The opening chapel service went well. My students helped put the folding chairs away. Then together—32 curious students and their rookie teacher—we walked to our classroom. It was an orderly procession. Books were distributed. I sat on my teaching stool in the front of the room and talked a little about myself. I told them about my teaching goals for the year and what I was expecting of them. They listened respectfully. Then we played a game so I could get to know them better.

Things were going well. I looked down at my plan for the day. Next on the list was recess. I glanced at the clock. That's when the sinking feeling struck. Recess wasn't scheduled for another hour. I had used only 30 minutes. I looked at the class. All 32 pairs of eyes stared back. I felt like Alice shrinking in Wonderland. It was the beginning of the longest day of my life.

Change can sometimes be overwhelming. You feel like you are in over your head and there is no way out, nothing to hold on to. Keeping afloat takes all of your energy.

But, with 20/20 hindsight, I can now see the tremendous blessings of that first-day experience. Right from the start I knew I needed help just to survive. Since praying is very comfortable for me (a habit from childhood), I started there. "Our help is in the name of the LORD, the Maker of heaven and earth" (Psalm 124).

Paul: a model for change

There are plenty of examples in the Bible of people who felt overwhelmed, who were in over their heads. Peter literally had to tread water. Jonah got wet too. Moses had a group much larger than 32. And Paul started with impossible odds of succeeding in his mission.

Paul wanted to serve. He was a zealous worker. His training was in Jewish law. Paul, first known as Saul, was a young man on a mission. Acts chapter 8 describes his mission as hateful and personal, aimed at ridding the world of those who put their faith in Jesus. We are told, "Saul began to destroy the church." But his murderous threats were silenced when the light of understanding was turned on. Jesus himself asked Saul, "Why do you persecute me?" Saul was stunned by the guilt of his own faulty understandings. The faith planted in his heart by his Savior transformed Saul, an enemy of God's people, to Paul, zealous missionary for Christ's church.

Paul's task seemed overwhelming. He had to convince the followers of Jesus that he was working with them, not against them. In his own mysterious way, the Lord spoke on Paul's behalf: "This man is my chosen instrument to carry my name before the Gentiles and their kings and before the people of Israel. I will show him how much he must suffer for my name" (Acts 9).

My second day of teaching went much better than my first. Armed with prayer, a sense of calm replaced the anxieties of the previous day. I had learned that I didn't have to know everything to teach 13-year-olds. I didn't even have to convince them that I could do the job. I was there to teach, to serve the Lord. I was willing and eager. God would do the rest. "In all your ways acknowledge him, and he will make your paths straight" (Proverbs 3:6).

After Paul's conversion he immediately went to work, serving his Lord. The Bible says, "At once he began to preach in the synagogues that Jesus is the Son of God."

There was a conspiracy to kill Paul. That didn't stop him. He traveled to Jerusalem where he continued to speak boldly in the name of the Lord. In fact, wherever Paul went he continued to preach Christ crucified. His crooked path was made straight.

Today I can look back and see how much I grew during that first year in teaching. The more I leaned, the more God held me up. I learned that *trust* means to give up your own understandings and let God be in charge. I learned to go forward with boldness and confidence, even when your students are taller than you are.

On the last day of that same school year, you would barely have been able to pick me out of the crowd. I am the one sitting on a regular classroom chair, completely surrounded by my students. They study my face as I open the gift card. The comfortable silence is punctuated by twitters and giggles. The messages and signatures blur as I read. Then I unwrap the gift box. Inside is a delicate string of 32 pearls—one for each member of my class.

A new family

A gentle breeze wafts the sweet scent of jasmine through the window. It grows alongside a small strip of well-watered grass. Everything else visible fits into the category of "concrete jungle."

The words *condo* and *southern California* usually evoke images of warm sandy beaches and tanned bodies. Actually, our condo was more like a two-bedroom apartment, and this area of California had a lot of dirt, noise, cars, people, and smog.

Moving to California brought change. Huge change. But the change in geography wasn't nearly as profound as having a baby. Practically overnight we went from two incomes and a quaint house with a garden to one income, an increase in rent, and another mouth to feed. But there were actually some things in this dramatic turn of events that we later learned to welcome. For one, there was a certain simplicity to our new California lifestyle. Having a baby actually meant slowing down. Daily life now typically revolved around bath time, laundry (especially those cloth diapers), mealtime, naptime, grocery shopping, and rocking. There was a peaceful rhythm to my new life. And in spite of its constant demands, I found freedom in its regularity.

Oh, there were times when I wished husbands could breast-feed too, at least between the hours of midnight and 5 A.M. My husband is blessed with acute hearing. He will wake at the slightest noise during the night. But for some strange reason, he could sleep through crying at any decibel level. The next morning he would grin and observe, "He slept through!" Mark didn't learn until our third child that there was probably a better way to ask how my night had been.

Still, I have to wonder why it is that so many women in our society see motherhood only as an endless procession of unrewarding tasks. To them, washing dirty diapers and feeding a tiny human every few hours doesn't sound very important. Why is that? How can something as beautiful as motherhood become such a lowly endeavor?

After gaining confidence in my instincts as a mother, the attachment—an infant's complete dependence—gave me a wonderful feeling of self-worth and importance. It was fascinating to watch the development of this young life. Each day brought something new—hours spent in "conversations," imitating each other's facial expressions, "reading" stacks of books and magazines together, walks not for exercise, but at the rate of an inquisitive ten-month-old. Everything was new and exciting. Everything was fresh, even in the concrete jungle. Life was rich and full. It was easy to see how God was blessing us.

I was still teaching. My home was the classroom. My own children were the students. When I balanced my children on my lap at the piano, singing simple hymns, they learned love. When I dragged the load of diapers down to wash and laughed as we had conversations sitting on top of the vibrating washing machine, they learned love. When I took those quiet evening walks outside to undo the day's tension, I taught love. When I responded with a quiet gentle voice to the loud cries, I taught love. When we read from picture books and Bible story books, they learned love. When we sang fun songs and "Jesus Loves Me," they learned love. When we visited Great Gramma or gathered flowers for the elderly lady down the street, they learned love.

The books and articles I read about the development of children all stress that most of the things a child learns are acquired by imitation. As the parent of young, impressionable minds, I took the words of Ephesians chapter 5 to heart: "Be imitators of God, therefore, as dearly loved children and live a life of love, just as Christ loved us and gave himself up for us as a fragrant offering and sacrifice to God." And 1 Corinthians chapter 13 gives a whole list of the love lessons I need to imitate in my own life and teach to my children by personal example: "Love is patient, love is kind. It does not envy, it does not boast, it is not proud. It is not rude, it is not self-seeking, it is not easily angered, it keeps no record of wrongs. Love does not delight in evil but rejoices with the truth. It always protects, always trusts, always hopes, always perseveres. Love never fails."

A new direction

Change can be very stressful. But it can also make a person grow.

We moved again . . . to Minnesota, where there is an abundance of heat and mosquitoes. My husband was doing his graduate work. To supplement our income, Mark found various jobs, tending bar or washing UPS trucks. He left early in the morning for class, returned for supper, then left again for work. He got home very late and studied. We lived in three rooms in his parents' home . . . and had another baby. The house was packed with people—five adults and two children under the age of two—all gathered around the table, saying their prayers before supper.

But another kind of change, even more earth shattering, was coming.

A specialist said there were no tumors. The tests showed no cause for the massive brain seizures (*grand mal* was the term he used). But I would have to give up my driver's license. And for at least two years, I would have to take a new medication to control the unexplainable seizures.

The drug's side effects made me unsure of myself. My hands refused to cooperate with my head and shook with uncertainty. I got dizzy walking around the corner in the hallway. And my greatest fear was that I would drop our three-month-old daughter. Talk about slowing down!

It was easy to become absorbed in self-pity. I started my days contemplating life's unfairness with my morning cup of coffee. Sometimes I needed a good shaking like a bathroom rug. But my contemplation always ended up back at the same question: "What is the Lord trying to teach me this time?"

David, whose life was filled with contemplation, wrote, "My times are in your hands" (Psalm 31:15). What a beautiful picture—the Lord wrapping his gentle hands around "my times"!

During the years in Minnesota, my husband, the avid bird-watcher, volunteered to help band bluebirds. He took along our son, who was almost three at the time. Decked out in matching vests, with pockets for everything from field guides to pliers, the two set out on the bluebird trail.

Each bluebird box was opened and the contents recorded. Any bluebird chicks would be gently scooped out and banded.

My husband's large hands encompassed each bluebird as he gently put it into our son's chubby fingers. As our son wrapped his small hands around the soft, fuzzy baby, Mark would say, "Be gentle. Don't squeeze." Our son held so still, mimicking the tenderness of his father.

The expression "My times are in your hands" leaves me with that kind of picture. Not a forceful hand pulling me up, but the gentle hands of an almighty God wrapped around me, carrying me through moments like this in my life. Protecting me.

Paul's hardships

The apostle Paul had trying times in his life. In 2 Corinthians chapter 12, he shares some of his sufferings and afflictions. From what the Bible tells us, his greatest hardship was personal—a disease, a crippling condition, a weakness—we don't really know the actual nature of his struggle. We only know that he must have struggled mightily with his affliction. "Three times I pleaded with the Lord to take it from me. But he said to me, 'My grace is sufficient for you, for my power is made perfect in weakness.' Therefore I will boast all the more gladly about my weaknesses, so that Christ's power may rest on me. That is why, for Christ's sake, I delight in weaknesses, in insults, in hardships, in persecutions, in difficulties. For when I am weak, then I am strong." Those words of Paul were a powerful source of encouragement for me during the difficult times I faced.

There was a hidden beauty to be found in my own weaknesses. In my forced slowdown, my horizons expanded. I began to write. In an effort to get my head and hands coordinated, I sat more hours at the piano, playing the music I loved. Painting and knitting calmed my shaking hands. I grew inside as I cared for our children, finding new strength in my dependence on a gentle, caring God. "Praise be to the LORD, for he has heard my cry for mercy. The LORD is my strength and my shield; my heart trusts in him, and I am helped" (Psalm 28:6,7).

A return

It is a hot day today, the first day of a new school year. The scenery has changed once again. We are living in the great Northwest. Weather this hot is a bit unusual. Life has once again taken a dramatic turn.

Our children have grown. Oh, how they've grown! For the first time in 14 years, I am going back to work full-time. Feeling totally inadequate, I have now joined the ranks of moms who take care of their families, cook, clean, and work a full day "out there" for pay.

The new challenge in life is to try to keep up with the questions of 27 five-, six-, and seven-year-olds. My voice is strained. There is always one talking, another asking questions, one in front of me, and a little train of them behind me. If I back up, I will undoubtedly step on someone, and they will all tumble down like dominoes.

My eyes were wide open as I stepped back into full-time teaching, unlike my first day in the classroom 20 years earlier. My goals were simpler this time, not for me but for my students. They would learn to read (voraciously, I hoped), be willing to write about anything, share their curiosity about the way things worked, and enjoy the puzzlement of math. They would sing from their hearts and be open to new ideas. They would love learning. And they would grow in their love and appreciation for their Savior.

But I was not ready for this.

My husband walked into my classroom at the end of that first day, smiling. He asked, "Well, how did it go?"

Not even lifting my head from my hands, I just croaked, "I wrote on the brand new white board with permanent markers."

Sometimes change can be very complex. It has a way of creating a ripple effect, affecting many people in a variety of ways. In this case, my family experienced the change more profoundly than I did. My returning to the classroom full-time effectively slammed the door on "mom's business hours." They had to become more like that little train of students that followed everywhere behind me, patiently waiting their turn.

Patience was the main ingredient. Like the glue spilled out in abundance on first grade assignments, patience would hold everything together. I needed extra patience as a teacher so there would be leftovers as a mom. The members of my family also needed an extra measure of patience as their comfort zone at home took on new dimensions. And I needed patience with myself. I still wanted life to remain orderly. I wanted things to go smoothly, both at home and at school.

Patience can be as elusive as matching socks in an almost empty dryer. Just when you think everything will match up, some leftover appears and your plans don't fit together. My "socks" usually didn't match up at the end of the day. A slight mishap would send me over the cliff into a free fall. Time and again I would end up mired in the slime and the muck of "Because I said so!" Time and again I would find myself praying, "Lord, please fill me with a plentiful supply of patience." At the same time, the same prayer began to echo from family members during our family devotions at home: "Please, Lord, give Mom more patience."

David's life of change

The Bible teems with examples of the kind of change that has this ripple effect on the lives of others. Think of Ruth, who decided to stay with an embittered Naomi. The changes in Ruth's life brought her to the attention of her future husband, shaping the future of many generations. Those changes thrust Ruth, a Moabitess, into the very heart of the ancestral succession leading to the arrival on earth of God's Messiah.

Think of Naaman's young servant girl. Her courage brought healing to a man whose leprosy threatened not only his health but the well-being of his family and those in his hire. Think of those fishermen who pulled their boats up on shore and left everything to follow Jesus. Or the jailer at Philippi, who brought Paul and Silas into his home, where he and the other members of his family were baptized.

Jesus' ancestor King David had forwarding addresses ranging from pasture to palace to dark caves. It was a patient David who wrote: "I waited patiently for the LORD; he turned to me and heard my cry. He lifted me out of the slimy pit, out of the mud and mire; he set my feet on a rock and gave me a firm place to stand" (Psalm 40:1,2).

Teaching should not be compared to a slimy pit. Neither should the tasks of cooking and doing laundry be compared to mud and mire. But my prayers were answered; the Lord provided the stepping stones I needed when I needed them.

Future years will, no doubt, bring plenty of their own changes. I'm almost certain there will be new reasons for prayers and pleas for an extra supply of patience. I've learned that it's the changes that happen *in* us, not those that happen *to* us, that seem to produce the most interesting results. That is what I patiently look for now when I am confronted with change. In fact, I pray for it, because inside change means there is real growth taking place. It is inside, in our hearts, where we connect with Jesus, the vine, to receive his sustenance. Only with his nurture can we begin to bear fruit. "If you remain in me and my words remain in you," Jesus said, "ask whatever you wish, and it will be given you. This is to my Father's glory, that you bear much fruit, showing yourselves to be my disciples" (John 15:7,8).

Now, that's real change!

CHAPTER FIVE

Cocoa-Covered Footprints

The kitchen floor hadn't really needed sweeping until Katherine mixed up a batch of cookies. And I hadn't really planned on doing housework. Instead, I wanted to do a few *special* things—things I never otherwise find the time for. After fighting the weeds in the garden, I was hoping to reward myself with a few hours at my art table. I love to paint. But there I was sweeping the kitchen floor.

I glanced down. The broom was making a mess instead of a clean sweep. Bits of butter were sticking to the bristles. A greasy film coated parts of the floor next to the powdery film of cocoa. As I knelt down to wipe up the butter, I noticed something unusual about the film of cocoa powder in the part I had already swept. Some had remained in the shape of . . . no, it couldn't be . . . footprints! I laughed at the irony— something so sweet in the disguise of an ugly chore! Her shoes must have been sticky before she used the cocoa powder. Even then I marveled at the fine job Katherine had done of mixing those cookies.

She had wanted to bake cookies two days earlier, but we didn't have peanut butter chips in the house. This morning she had asked again.

"Okay," I agreed. "But I'm going to do my own work. I won't be in the kitchen to help you. And [I paused for emphasis] you have to clean up the counter and take care of the dishes."

She was so pleased. Not only did she have permission to bake cookies; she was in charge of the whole kitchen.

She only came to the window to ask for help twice. Once to measure the butter, and a second time to ask about the "dry in-gre-di-ents." I reminded her to use the mixer carefully at a slow speed.

"And keep the beaters down while it's turned on," I called to her. I remember wondering if she heard me. But I was confident she knew how to keep her fingers and the spatula out of the bowl while the mixer was running.

So Katherine mixed. And I pulled weeds. We were both busy in our own worlds and with our own projects for a long time.

When she was done, Katherine asked if she could go across the street to play with her friends. I reminded her about cleaning up.

She was gone in a flash, returning a few minutes later. "All done," she grinned. "Can I go now?"

That's when I returned to the house to check on her progress.

Lumps of chocolate cookie dough were stuck on spoons and several measuring cups lay in the sink. I guess that could qualify as "taking care of the dishes." I had a hunch the recipe for four dozen would not see its full yield. The kitchen counter, mixer, and walls had sort of a paisley look where the cocoa powder and flour had settled. That's probably why I didn't notice the floor at first. She had hurriedly cleaned the counter, as agreed, then happily rushed out the door. The paisley walls, the sink full of dishes, and the cocoa-covered footprints were left for me.

There is a melancholy in the happiness of watching your youngest child grow. As a mother teaches and guides through each new milestone, she knows it will be the last time. I remember feeling that way when our youngest started taking her first steps. I even felt that way when she gave up breast-feeding, and I once again gained my freedom. I reminisced about her first words and her awkward sentences that turned into nonstop conversations.

I thought of our older children, marveling at their independence and accomplishments. Each of us is on his or her own learning curve.

Then, quite suddenly, I felt humbled as I realized the depth of God's love for our family. The blessings were too numerous to count. Some were even hard to recognize as blessings. There were days when a mess like the one on our kitchen floor would have appeared monumental—days when a filthy floor would have seemed so unfair. Instead of the cocoa-covered footprints I would have noticed my sore knees and tired back. How *we've* grown!

"How To" be a parent

The more I grow, I am convinced, the less I know. The older I become, the more I realize how much there is to learn. In my spiritual life, the more I study the Scriptures, the more I want to know. I find myself searching, asking questions (but not questions about my faith). My salvation is as sure to me as the dawning of a new day. But the more I read the Scriptures, the more insight I receive for living my life. I am more capable to handle my everyday tasks. Maybe, like those footprints, these daily readings serve as tangible evidence that I have grown.

Chapter 3 in Colossians is one of those places in Scripture to which I often return during times like this one, scrubbing instead of painting. Once upon a time it would have produced a different attitude regarding my task. Anger and frustration would have gotten the floor scrubbed quickly but not clean enough for me. Instead of the sweet smell and delicious taste of the cookies, I would have focused on the sour taste of my anger. It would have spilled out on anyone near, usually our children. Colossians puts it bluntly into a godly perspective: "Since, then, you have been raised with Christ, set your hearts on things above, where Christ is seated at the right hand of God. Set your minds on things above, not on earthly things. . . . Put to death, therefore, whatever belongs to your earthly nature. . . . You used to walk in these ways, in the life you once lived. But now you must rid yourselves of all such things as these: anger, rage, malice, slander, and filthy language from your lips."

Anger can be a devastating emotion. But it can also be curbed. Frustrations can be controlled.

I had a chance to practice *curbing* my anger the day one of our children discovered a fascination with scissors. The cutting was done very scientifically. Different materials were systematically inspected and experimented on. In a single day, a sibling's hair, the living room drapes, and a treasured afghan were tested against the power of a child's safety scissors, no less. As the day wore on and more experiments were discovered, my anger mounted and my words became cutting.

Later that day I attended a meeting with close friends, fellow volunteers at a pregnancy counseling center. The topic was "How to help young mothers." As we sat down, we each received a bookmark entitled "Twelve Ways to Avoid Disciplining in Anger." A friend, who knew about the scissors incidents, roared with laughter at the look on my face. She restyled the bookmark to fit my needs: "Twelve Ways to Avoid Disciplining a Scissors Artist in Anger." Then she howled with laughter again. Sometimes the Lord has to use a two-by-four to get our attention. Or a roaring friend.

A Christian mother's wardrobe

Colossians chapter 3 not only provides the most excellent way for a Christian parent to approach the topic of discipline, it also gives us guidelines to live by. "Therefore, as God's chosen people, holy and dearly loved, clothe yourselves with compassion, kindness, humility, gentleness and patience. Bear with each other and forgive whatever grievances you may have against one another. Forgive as the Lord forgave you. And over all these virtues put on love, which binds them all together in perfect unity."

Every day brings its own set of troubles and challenges. My shortcomings tag right along. Yet, by faith in Jesus, I am still one of God's chosen people, forgiven by his blood. I am holy in his sight. And I am dearly loved, and fully forgiven, by God.

There is a thick book on my shelf entitled *The Book of Virtues,* by William J. Bennett. The author has listed ten key virtues and provided literary examples of each one. In his attempts to "aid in the time-honored task of the moral education of the young," Bennett points out that this book "should help us lift our eyes." Inside the front cover of my copy, these cherished words are written: "To Mom for your 38th birthday," followed by three signatures in a variety of handwritings showing different levels of maturity. The signatures are in pen. They will not be erased, a constant reminder of Mr. Bennett's words: "If we want our children to possess the traits of character we most admire, we need to teach them what those traits are and why they deserve both admiration and allegiance."

Take Ruth, for example

Compassion. Kindness. Humility. Gentleness. Patience. The Old Testament model of Ruth comes readily to mind.

Ruth married into a family from Bethlehem. This family had come to Moab to escape a drought in their homeland. During their stay in Moab, the men in the family died. The young widow, Ruth, returned with her embittered mother-in-law to Bethlehem. The stage was set for Ruth, who filled the role of a virtuous woman when life seemed to be stacked against her.

The Bible provides no background for Ruth as a young girl. We cannot study her upbringing. It has left out any mention of her family and any previous influences in her life. But we do get some insight into the influence that a godly Naomi, and her family, must have had on Ruth. When Ruth was faced with making a decision on taking a new direction of profound sacrifice in her life, there was no lack of commitment or faith. This is what Ruth said to old Naomi: "Your people will be my people and your God my God."

Ruth's statement was one of no small amount of conviction. She saw herself as one of God's chosen people, holy and dearly loved. Returning to a foreign land with a bitter old woman, Ruth clothed herself in more than a widow's rags. Even with her heavy burden, she was cloaked in the virtues found in Colossians.

Ruth's compassion is evident. Ruth clung to her mother-in-law saying, "Don't urge me to leave you or to turn back from you." Ruth did not think of herself first. Instead, she was sympathetic to Naomi's needs. Ruth was even willing to leave her own country, to be a stranger in a new land, just to care for Naomi.

Ruth's kindness was shown when she pleaded with Naomi, "Let me go to the fields and pick up the leftover grain behind anyone in whose eyes I find favor." This kindness that Ruth offered came with risk. As a stranger, a foreigner (a Moabitess, no less), Ruth, no doubt, suffered from the prejudices of the local population in Bethlehem. But Ruth didn't mind what others said or thought about her. She willingly worked hard. And she was noticed for the great kindness she showed to Naomi.

The Lord watched over her. His guiding hand became evident when Ruth met Boaz.

Ruth's humility is noticeable in the way she spoke to Boaz: "You have given me comfort and have spoken kindly to your servant—though I do not have the standing of one of your servant girls." A Moabitess was not very high on the social ladder. Ruth humbly accepted his generosity.

Ruth's gentleness and patience can be seen throughout the book. Her gentleness was evident as she wept, hugging Naomi. It can be seen in the quiet and discreet way she lay at the feet of Boaz on the threshing floor. Her gentleness was not timid, but determined. It did not demand anything in return. What gentle patience Ruth displayed for a bitter Naomi, who called herself *empty,* even in Ruth's company! How patiently Ruth accepted what each new day would bring!

Ruth's life did not unfold by chance or coincidence. God's guiding hand is evident throughout the book. Ruth and Boaz were in God's plans from the beginning of time. And his blessings were to be found in everything from the handfuls of barley to their new little baby named Obed.

And put on love

The screen door bangs just as the last pan of cookies comes out of the oven. "Hey Mom! What's that smell? Are those my cookies? Did I do a good job mixing them?"

Our daughter with the nonstop conversations has grown. She is becoming a beautiful young lady. Her cooking skills have grown with her independence. When the cocoa powder settled this time, she had a bit more confidence in her abilities. But she still has room to grow. Yes, we still need to work on those cleaning skills.

The book about virtues points out "that there is nothing more influential, more determinant, in a child's life than the moral power of quiet example." Another good reason to pray for patience! Pray for the patience to be that quiet example to your offspring—the kind of godly virtue that doesn't avoid a situation in order not to deal with it or scream in anger to get a point across.

I have learned to hope that our children are able to weed out the times when my focus is not clear, the times I respond in anger. If my lessons to them regarding patience have been effective, they will forgive me also when I have been impatient.

My garden finally got weeded. The painting finally happened. The cookies are gone. I see it all as a growing process . . . for me . . . for our daughter . . . for the whole family. This is how we learn to live the Christian life. "And over all these virtues put on love, which binds them all together in perfect unity." Therein lies the richness of God's bountiful blessings, a gift for the taking. His love for us is transformed into our love for one another. All things considered, that is quite a miracle.

CHAPTER SIX

The Cat in the Cupboard

It wasn't really a prenuptial agreement. I never did say yes to that part. When Mark said "No diapers and no cats," I just grinned.

The first cat was all black, a present for my husband's birthday from my sister. "Tomorrow that cat goes to the pound," he said. She cried. He looked at me. "We agreed. No cats!" I wasn't grinning.

Somehow Toby was allowed to stay. Toby was definitely Mark's cat. Feisty. Mean. And scared of most things. Toby slept in Mark's desk drawer.

A year passed. I pointed out that Toby needed company. Mark reminded me of the alleged agreement. We bantered over semantics.

Finally I asked, "What if I find one that is all white, short haired, and free? A complete opposite, like salt and pepper." He seemed to agree, though he says now that he doesn't remember.

A couple weeks later, Mark left for summer school. When he returned, there was Percy, a cute white kitten, pouncing on everything that moved—Toby's tail included.

Toby was disgusted. My husband agreed that if the kitten could survive Toby for the next week, we'd keep him.

Percy stayed for 15 years. With the nickname Frank Burns, he never really seemed intelligent. But he feared neither man nor beast . . . until the day we moved.

43

One evening, while dining with friends, we had a conversation about living in different parts of the country. My husband remarked, "I'd never live in southern California." That very night he received a call to teach in North Hollywood. A few short months later, we were moving.

The day the van came, we shut the cats in a back room so they would be safely out of the way. At the end of the day, we let them out again. The house was completely empty, except for our sleeping bags and suitcases.

Poor Percy! His eyes widened. He crouched, walking slowly, fearfully, staying close to the walls. When calming him down didn't work, we went to sleep.

In the middle of the night, we woke to the sounds of an eerie moan. I don't believe in ghosts, but the sound gave me goose bumps. We got up to investigate. In the farthest corner of an open cupboard, two luminous circles stared back, while the unearthly sound continued. His body went limp as we picked him up. He dropped like a wet towel on a sleeping bag and cowered there. The rest of the night was punctuated by a series of moans, spooking Toby and stealing our precious sleep.

It was fear. Heart-stopping, paralyzing fear.

I don't live with much fear, but the memories of times in my life when I was genuinely afraid occasionally return with unsettling clarity. Like that first time on the high dive. I never have liked high places. To climb up on purpose seemed insane. But the instructor said, "Jump off and swim to the other end." My unwilling feet inched their way to the end of the board. Each step closer put more spring in the board and, in turn, amplified the shaking in my legs. I looked past my toes, groaning with prayer, trying not to fall, realizing I had to. I bent my knees, the board also bent, and then I was airborne. I shut my eyes tight and let the feeling envelop me, knowing that it would all end very soon.

Childbirth also comes to mind. One has no control over the situation. You can't turn around and change your mind or even postpone it for a while. "Excuse me, but I think I'll come back tomorrow." My rational mind was in complete rebellion as I tried to reason: "This too will end. You can get through this. Just take it one moment at a time."

Yet, fear intrigues us.

Childbirth is also a good example of our fascination with fear. Just get a room full of women together and bring up the subject of childbirth. The whole character of the room changes. A quiet group turns vibrant with conversation. It's sharing time. And not until each has had an opportunity to talk her way through some horrible episode does the room settle down again with the relief of laughter. A fear that is defeated is a great accomplishment. Until the next time anyway.

Personal fears

Some of our greatest fears have to do with self-image. Remember those high school years? The world seemed to revolve around the moments when one's ego would either be fed or trashed, and life itself seemed to hang in the balance. I tried hard not to stumble over my own feet. I thought the ground would open up and swallow me if I tried to speak to someone I admired. So I usually retreated, tongue-tied, the words were never spoken.

This kind of fear can last well beyond one's high school days. The first time I had to speak to a large group reminded me of what fear can do. I had thought my speech through well in advance. Preparation meant nothing the instant I stood up. Instead, I was left with shaking extremities and a voice that squeaked with uncertainty. "Hello. My name is . . . (pause, to try to remember) Rachel." Not the confident image I wanted to present.

Peter's fears

A lot of people can relate to Peter. Bold Peter. Impetuous Peter. Fearful Peter. Picture Peter shouting "Lord, save me!" as his paralyzing fear pulled him down in those waves.

A composite of the gospel accounts found in Matthew chapter 4 and Luke chapter 5 gives us a good picture of how Peter came to follow the master: As Jesus was walking beside the Sea of Galilee, he saw at the water's edge two boats left by fishermen. There, washing their nets, were two brothers: Simon, called Peter, and his brother Andrew. They were casting a net into the lake, for they were fishermen.

You can almost hear the gentle waves lapping at Peter's boat as he cares for his nets. Jesus purposefully stopped there to preach, getting Peter's attention.

When Jesus had finished speaking, he said to Simon, "Put out into deep water and let down the nets for a catch." This is the beginning of a miracle. In this situation, one immediately recognizes two things about Peter: his willing obedience ("Because you say so, I will let down the nets") and his open-hearted, honest response when he witnessed the miraculous catch of fish. He fell at Jesus' feet and said, "Go away from me, Lord; I am a sinful man!"

We see Peter's quickness to respond. But his reactions were often not thought out in advance. Maybe that is the reason why his fears are so visible. "Go away," he said. He was sincerely aware of his shortcomings: "I am a sinful man!"

Peter's throat was dry and he was shaking as he contemplated his own imperfection. He dreaded the thought of having his sins exposed to God. But, like so many of us, he took the wrong tack, imploring Jesus to *leave him*.

Looking into Peter's soul, Jesus saw that Peter needed his unconditional love more than anything else. And now he was about to demonstrate both his love and his power to Peter in a most extraordinary way. "Don't be afraid; from now on you'll be fishers of men." Peter was being prompted. The teaching had begun. Peter's shortcomings had already been accepted, his sins forgiven.

A few years hence Peter would hear these words from Jesus again. It would happen when Jesus was preparing his disciples for his last days on earth. They were about to experience mind-bending confusion, and their confidence would, no doubt, be shaken to its foundation. So to comfort them and sustain them through this difficult time, Jesus said, "Peace I leave with you; my peace I give you. I do not give to you as the world gives. Do not let your hearts be troubled and do not be afraid" (John 14:27). The words *don't be afraid* must have echoed in Peter's heart for the rest of his natural life.

Living through fear

What beautiful words to calm a troubled soul! They help us remember, *I am a child of God, holy in his sight.* Even with my shortcomings, my doubts, my fears, he says *to me,* "Do not let your heart be troubled and do not be afraid." He promises me his peace, his presence, his help in every trouble.

This does not mean that all our troubles will go away. Hardly. Painful things will happen. My heart still beats rapidly and my voice quavers when I have to speak in public. But the peace is there, waiting. "Call upon me in the day of trouble; I will deliver you, and you will honor me" (Psalm 50:15). This is God's promise.

It is good for parents to remember that the fears children experience, though sometimes quite irrational, are still very real to them. I still can picture the details of the parking lot where I learned to ride my bike. When I froze in fear and wiped out, even my cheeks were scraped. I can also remember hiding in a closet so I wouldn't have to go get my immunization shots. I should have remembered those times when I spent the evening in the bathroom with our son.

It was just a loose tooth. His first. He could bend it all the way forward with his tongue, but he couldn't push it out. It held on by one small piece of flesh. The sharp edges irritated the surrounding gums. So Dan decided he wouldn't eat. By suppertime my patience had melted, exposing raw resolve. "After supper we are going into that bathroom, and we are not coming out until that tooth is out of your mouth!" I said, with all the patience I could still muster.

He could tell from my tone that this was the end of life as he knew it.

Elizabeth's eyes were glowing with excitement. She was really looking forward to this. "Will there be any blood?" she asked.

After we gave thanks for supper, we left the dishes and headed into the bathroom. I got out cotton swabs, ice, and a washcloth. Everything was laid out next to the sink. Elizabeth's eyes grew bigger. She was mentally recording all of this for future reference. Then I said, "Okay, Dan, I'm ready. Open up."

Every time my fingers got within three inches of his mouth, a warning would go off in the form of a blood-curdling scream. Then his mouth would clamp shut. Tight!

I talked in a calm tone. "Let me try just holding it without pulling. See? Just like this." I demonstrated on my teeth. We tried again. The scream was louder this time. I showed him how it would work, using his all-too-willing sister as a model. That resolved nothing. We explored all the other options and accessories. The scream continued.

It was a hot summer evening and the bathroom window was wide open. I wondered how long the neighbors would let the screaming go on before they called the police. "There's a woman torturing her children in the bathroom." An hour ticked by. My ears were beginning to hurt. Our daughter, patiently waiting for the blood, never left Dan's side. We made plans. We prayed. But the tooth simply wouldn't fall out.

After two hours, I thought it was good Dan would never have to experience childbirth.

I don't know what finally made him give it a try. Maybe his jaw hurt from clamping it shut so hard or so often. Maybe his throat was getting tired. For whatever reason he allowed me to put my fingers around the tooth as agreed. No pulling yet. Then he said okay and I pulled. With the slightest snapping sound, more felt than heard, the tooth came out. There wasn't even enough of a connection left to allow for any blood. His look was incredulous. I could read his thoughts: *You mean that's all there is to this?* With a "Whoop!" he was gone.

His sister looked dejected. "Where's all the blood?" she asked.

Fear of death

There are, of course, some fears that are quite understandable and justifiable. Fear of pain or death is pure instinct. In Matthew chapter 14, we're told that Peter went from the height of faith to the depths of this fear one night in the middle of the Sea of Galilee.

They had left Jesus behind. The master had had a hard day, first learning of John the Baptist's death, then preaching to and feeding a crowd of five thousand-plus hungry people. The disciples were halfway across the lake when they saw Jesus walking on the water. But they didn't recognize him. They thought it was a ghost, so they were terrified, likely fearing for their lives.

Jesus immediately addressed their fear: "Take courage! It is I. Don't be afraid." The same words, the same lake. Jesus must have had Peter's attention now. But this situation was a little different from that earlier encounter. Instead of Peter trying to send Jesus away, he said, "Lord, if it's you, tell me to come to you on the water."

When Jesus offered an invitation, "Peter got down out of the boat, walked on the water and came toward Jesus. But when he saw the wind, he was afraid and, beginning to sink, cried out, 'Lord, save me!'" Peter's logic won out over faith. His trust was replaced with panic as he sank.

I don't like flying. I understand the principles behind lift and thrust. I also see the safety in the statistics of flying compared to driving. I still don't like flying. A recent flight back to the Midwest was smooth, the scenery beautiful, until we came to the Wisconsin border. (Only later did I learn that there had been tornado warnings on the ground.) As our plane made its final approach, we were stunned by the sight of Chicago—flooded, immobilized. Then suddenly it felt like we were on a wild roller-coaster ride. (I don't like roller coasters either.) My logic pointed out that this was not normal, and I reached for my own "panic button."

This is how my prayers were answered on that day. As that plane bounced through pockets of turbulent air, a warm calm flooded through me, reducing my fears to a level at which I could continue calmly praying. Chicago was a beautiful sight on that day.

As Jesus reached out to save Peter from the enveloping waves, he also gave Peter something to think about: "You of little faith, why did you doubt?" I need the same words every time I let panic rule my thoughts.

Less than a year later, Peter was shocked when Jesus explained that "he must go to Jerusalem and suffer many things at the hands of the elders, chief priests and teachers of the law, and that he must be killed and on the third day be raised to life" (Matthew 16). Bold Peter had recently been honored for confessing, "You are the Christ, the Son of the living God." And Jesus had said, "Blessed are you, Simon son of Jonah . . . you are Peter, and on this rock I will build my church."

Peter loved his Lord. He didn't want to lose him. He couldn't imagine Jesus suffering and dying. In his fear he could neither comprehend nor accept losing Jesus. "Never, Lord!" was Peter's reaction.

Now Jesus spoke with a different tone in his voice. This time Jesus' words were harsh. "Get behind me, Satan! You are a stumbling block to me; you do not have in mind the things of God, but the things of men." Jesus' words slashed at Peter's heart. But they were true not only for Peter. The dark side of every one of us would prefer to have us wrapped up in our own human emotions and human logic instead of hoping and trusting in God's promises. A stumbling block for sure to the workings of his Spirit in our lives!

I know someone who is hesitant to pursue Christ crucified with a dying relative. Wayward for most of his adult life, this person is about to meet his Maker. Yet my friend hesitates to share the message of forgiveness and hope. Why?

I have friends who take their Lord as a possibility, a convenience when needed. Friends who question the wisdom of God in daily circumstances, blaming God for the disasters that result from sin. Why do I hesitate to speak to them with boldness about their Savior? I am no different than Peter in his fears. I need the same reprimand, the same direction.

Calming our fears

At the incredible transfiguration of Jesus, Peter went from the thrill of seeing Moses and Elijah with a transfigured Lord Jesus to instant terror. God's voice boomed from a cloud saying, "This is my Son, whom I love; with him I am well pleased. Listen to him!" (Matthew 17). When Peter, James, and John heard this, they fell to the ground in utter terror.

"But Jesus came and touched them. 'Get up,' he said. 'Don't be afraid.'" How wonderful that touch must have felt in the depths of their fear!

That touch makes me think of the times when our children have had nightmares. Going into their rooms and talking usually isn't enough to calm them. They need the touch of reality to take away their fears. A soothing hug. Holding their hands. Giving them back rubs. This provides physical reassurance and relieves their frightened thoughts. Grown-ups sometimes need that same reassurance.

My Savior, the Good Shepherd, does that for me. When my unexplainable fears surface, I find the Shepherd reaching out to me through his Word. His gentle hand points to the answers I need for my life. "He restores my soul. He guides me in paths of righteousness" (Psalm 23). Then his Spirit strengthens me with understanding. My faith grows. Other times his guiding hand touches my shoulder, gently leading me in his direction. "Your rod and your staff, they comfort me." Sometimes this touch is through other Christians who hold my hand, sit and talk with me, or pray for me. My fears subside. What a comfort touch can be! How simple it is to share it with others who are drowning in their own fears!

Peter was the one who boldly stood up and preached to the crowd gathered at Pentecost. The same Peter who hid by the fire, denying his Savior, was now strengthened by the Holy Spirit. With his fear removed, he was bold and confident. This is the Peter who later wrote: "Who is going to harm you if you are eager to do good? But even if you should suffer for what is right, you are blessed. 'Do not fear what they fear; do not be frightened.' But in your hearts set apart Christ as Lord. Always be prepared to give an answer to everyone who asks you to give the reason for the hope that you have" (1 Peter 3:13-15).

Peter learned from his fears and his mistakes. Guided by faith, he overcame those fears and moved on to serve his Lord, sharing what he had learned. The same Peter who sank in the waves shouting "Lord, save me!" later wrote: "Humble your-selves, therefore, under God's mighty hand, that he may lift you up in due time. Cast all your anxiety on him because he cares for you" (1 Peter 5:6,7).

Elizabeth never had to spend an evening in the bathroom with her first loose tooth. While eating rice for supper one night, she suddenly pulled a small white object from her mouth and exclaimed, "Look! My tooth!" And then she promptly put it back in and swallowed it.

As we rose from our chairs, gasping, "No! Don't!" she just giggled. Totally pleased with herself, she grinned triumphantly. There was her loose tooth, still attached to her gums. "Got ya!" she said.

A fear that is defeated is truly a great accomplishment.

CHAPTER SEVEN

You're on the Air!

Sitting in the radio studio made me nervous. Mikes and cords were everywhere. It wasn't the studio, though, that made my heart pound inside my chest. I could feel the surge of panic all the way to my fingertips.

"Sixty seconds," said a voice. "Everyone quiet, please!"

A man on the other side of the room picked up a microphone and paused; then, "Good evening. This is *Live, by George!*" We had heard the same familiar voice in our living room many evenings.

I glanced at our nine-year-old son. He was grinning, taking in all the commotion—the technology and drama.

The music of the first few musicians floated effortlessly out of their small fingers. The host, George Shangrow, coaxed them into conversation. When they nodded their answers in response, he laughed. The mirth was contagious.

Then it was Dan's turn. My heart stopped beating, my mind a blur. Could our son be nine already? Wasn't he just 18 months old, dragging his stepping stool out to the living room to conduct his favorite songs on the radio? I remember thinking, "Dan really does have a God-given talent." At the same time, I was humbled with the realization that I had very little to do with any of it. It was, as all things are, *a gift*. Psalm 139 praises God with the words: "For you created my inmost being; you knit me together in my mother's womb. I praise you because I am fearfully and wonderfully made; your works are wonderful, I know that full well." When Dan was knit in my womb, God had music on his mind.

As our son stepped around the tangle of cords and sat at the piano, I could see his intense concentration. I have always encouraged our children to try new things. Tonight was a new experience for me. I wasn't sure if I liked the emotions that went along with it. My hands were shaking.

Dan had worried about what he would have to say on the radio. He doesn't like to talk. The host made it easy for him, stretching the interview around the minimal answers my son left him to work with. Then it was time for Dan to play. His fingers spoke volumes. "Homework Blues" was the title of his composition. His worries about talking on the radio were unfounded; Dan communicated through his music.

It would be easy to get caught up in such a moment—to make myself an extension of God's gift to my son—to own him: "This is *my* son." I reminded myself again: his talents are from God, and there is a reason for this blessing. Ephesians 2:10 says, "We are God's workmanship, created in Christ Jesus to do good works, which God prepared in advance for us to do." I wondered what good works God had planned long ago that were now waiting for Dan to do.

God's plans for Joseph

As Joseph's brothers stood before him, quaking with fear, Joseph explained how God had taken their actions and turned them into good. "And now, do not be distressed and do not be angry with yourselves for selling me here, because it was to save lives that God sent me ahead of you . . . to preserve for you a remnant on earth and to save your lives by a great deliverance" (Genesis 45). When Joseph's coat was ripped off and dipped in blood, neither Joseph nor his brothers had any inkling of the good works that God had prepared in advance for Joseph's life.

But, oh, the agony of Joseph's earlier life! His brothers' hatred. Slavery. A false accusation by Potiphar's wife. Imprisonment. Joseph's story is a rags-to-riches tale; but how much suffering did God have Joseph endure along the way? Maybe some gifts don't come entirely free. And surely some gifts have a special measure of responsibility attached to them. I tried to put Dan's gift for music into perspective. The Bible story of Joseph and his brothers seemed to have some applications, but as I considered much of Joseph's life, it wasn't all that comforting.

Doors have opened unexpectedly for Dan. Doris and I were members of the same art guild. She also enjoyed painting with watercolors. One Saturday, while waiting for a meeting to begin, we chatted. In the course of the conversation, I shared how I was searching for advice for our son. I explained that Dan had had a bad year in school and his music wasn't progressing. He was in a slump, mentally and emotionally. Doris listened with interest.

A few days later I got a phone call from Doris. "Will you please consider allowing me to pay for piano lessons for your son at the Conservatory this summer? I've been talking to our neighbor who goes there. She's been telling me about a wonderful teacher." Out of the blue God opens doors and shows the way!

Joseph's life is a wonderful example of the words in Colossians 3:17, "Whatever you do, whether in word or deed, do it all in the name of the Lord Jesus, giving thanks to God the Father through him." Sold into Potiphar's house, Joseph had the responsibility of a slave. He carried out his service to the fullest possible measure. The time he spent in Potiphar's house was an education. He needed to learn that his place in life didn't really matter. Whatever the task, God was there, blessing Joseph, helping him carry out the good works set aside for him.

What did matter was that Joseph was doing his best to put God's gifts to good use—to be honest and upright about it. Galatians chapter 6 makes this clear: "Each one should test his own actions. Then he can take pride in himself, without comparing himself to somebody else, for each one should carry his own load."

The responsibility to develop one's talent isn't always an easy thing to translate into action. In the case of music, it translates into *practice.* Unending practice! Scales. Arpeggios. Theory. New music. Discipline. Parents get to share these gifts and responsibilities with their children. We get the privilege of driving to, and sitting through, endless lessons, recitals, and rehearsals. Just listening to all those hours of practice is a daily exercise in patience. Along with this comes a responsibility to encourage one's children to carry their own loads. The gifts are theirs, not their parents'. When they reach adulthood, the external motivation of a supportive parent should cease to be the driving force behind their talents. Their motivation to continue to use their talents and abilities to God's glory will then need to well up from some deeper source.

Using gifts God's way

A Christian's motivation for developing and using a God-given gift comes from the giver himself. By faith (a unique spiritual gift) we are strengthened to use our gifts. By faith we have meaning and purpose for what we do in life. And by faith we express our gratitude in praise and worship. In 1 Peter 4:10,11, we read: "Each one should use whatever gift he has received to serve others, faithfully administering God's grace in its various forms. If anyone speaks, he should do it as one speaking the very words of God. If anyone serves, he should do it with the strength God provides, so that in all things God may be praised through Jesus Christ. To him be the glory and the power for ever and ever. Amen."

During a long car ride in the dark of night, Dan and I talked about his choices for the future. His schooling would have to follow the direction of a future career, but he was not interested in competitions or performing as a career. I mentioned that sometimes even the most talented of musicians pursues another career simply because musicians generally do not earn an adequate income. He listened carefully, then quietly asked, "What do you want me to do, Mom?"

"Do what you want to do. Don't let money rule your decision. Whatever you choose, choose something you love doing—something you will still love doing when you are 40 or 50." That is the standard answer for our culture. A hundred years ago most parents were hardly in a position to offer so many sweeping options. A hundred years ago most parents would have said, "Get a job." End of discussion.

"No, Mom. That's not what I meant. I meant, What do *you* want me to do?"

I sat quietly, searching my own thoughts. The only sound was the tires on the pavement, beating in a constant throbbing pattern. Finally I responded, choosing my words very carefully. "God has given you a special gift. Use that talent. Don't set it aside, waiting to use it again someday. Develop it. Make it grow. However you use it, whether it is teaching, conducting, or composing, that is up to you." Then we talked about the parable of the talents.

Divine economics

Jesus told a story about a man going on a journey (Matthew 25). The man called his servants together and entrusted his property to them. The master divided talents among his servants in varying amounts. When the Bible uses the word *talent,* it means a unit of measure or an amount of money. Each servant received an amount "according to his ability." These varying amounts symbolize the gifts and talents that God distributes to the people of our world—believers and unbelievers alike. These gifts come with different kinds of *intelligences,* in differing quantities. In other words, the gifts God gives come in many different shapes and sizes. And the servants in this parable each used the talents entrusted to them in different ways. "The man who had received the five talents went at once and put his money to work and gained five more. So also, the one with the two talents gained two more. But the man who had received the one talent went off, dug a hole in the ground and hid his master's money."

Notice how the master knew to give more talents to the servants who made the most of their opportunity. He gave to each, "according to his ability." Such wisdom reaches beyond our reasoning or judgment. We don't question why we have a talent or why we can't do what others can. We simply use our God-given talents to the best of our abilities. A text in Romans chapter 12 explains it this way: "We have different gifts, according to the grace given us. If a man's gift is prophesying, let him use it in proportion to his faith. If it is serving, let him serve; if it is teaching, let him teach; if it is encouraging, let him encourage; if it is contributing to the needs of others, let him give generously; if it is leadership, let him govern diligently; if it is showing mercy, let him do it cheerfully."

The Lord also gives us the ability to carry out his plans. He promises to provide resources, such as prayer, to help us get the job done. Ask. Seek. Knock. And he cheers for our successes. "Well done, good and faithful servant! You have been faithful with a few things; I will put you in charge of many things." And, now, note the rewards: "Come and share in your master's happiness!"

Joseph refused to hide his talents. A hidden talent is the evidence of a certain amount of fear and uncertainty. When a talent has been hidden, something is missing. The thing that is missing is trust—trust in the giver of the gift.

Joseph surely was fearful on his journey to Egypt. But his fear did not keep him from trusting in the Lord God. This trust enabled him to do his work to God's glory. In doing so, he was blessed with more responsibilities. Joseph was like those servants in Jesus' parable who doubled their master's talents. And, having received much in return on his investment, Joseph was permitted to share in his master's happiness, even while he remained on earth.

When the Lord distributes special talents, he expects much in return. Conversely, selfish pride—the kind that says, "Look at me; see what I can do"—will paralyze a talented individual just as readily as fear. The apostle Paul puts our human inclination into a godly perspective: "By the grace given me I say to every one of you: Do not think of yourself more highly than you ought, but rather think of yourself with sober judgment, in accordance with the measure of faith God has given you" (Romans 12:3).

Serving is using the talents God has given us. In this Romans chapter, for example, notice all the different areas of gifts mentioned: prophesying, serving, teaching, encouraging, contributing, leading, and being merciful. But the Bible doesn't say that one person has to do all of these. God has created many people, and he distributes many gifts among them, expecting them to be used faithfully. But I don't have to cover the shortcomings of others. And I do not expect to be given a grand gift that lets me do it all. Instead, I accept the gift I get. Cheerfully. Joyfully. And I use it faithfully to the best of my own abilities, with the strength God gives me. Honestly. For God's glory alone.

Dan listened quietly that night as we made our way home. He asked a few pertinent questions until the conversation returned to its origin. Then I had one final chance to make a mother's feelings known, understanding that from that point on the decision would have to be Dan's. "No matter what career you take, whichever educational avenue you pursue, you must keep your faith as a top priority. It's your faith that gives you strength. Remember your confirmation passage, Philippians 4:13? 'I can do everything through him who gives me strength.' And because of your faith, you have a need to give back to the Lord. Not just money. You need to give back some of the talent he has given you in service to him, just like you are doing now by playing for chapel and accompanying choir. If you perform, play music in your church. If you end up composing, write some music for church choirs. Be like Bach who wrote *Soli Deo Gloria* right next to his own signature—'to God alone be the glory.'"

"I know, Mom. I will do that," he answered in his quiet tone. I knew that he was sincere in what he had just said. A mother knows. I knew also that our conversation was one of those turning points when a parent has just *let go*. How quickly the time of parental influence passes! Then our children are adults. Our time together is precious. I wondered sadly how far apart we would be separated in life.

God's timing is always best. I once joked that the Lord knew I needed to grow up some more before he gave us our first child. But there are many times when I still feel inadequate, as though I need to grow more before God moves me into another phase of life. I wondered if I was mature enough to really let go now that the time had apparently come.

CHAPTER EIGHT

A Journey into Stir-Fry and Beyond

I have always enjoyed Chinese food: tiny morsels of tantalizing tastes, delicate finger cups of delicious tea, and sweetly mysterious sauces. I remember going to a restaurant in Chinatown as a child. I was intrigued with each entree brought to the table. Each person received a brightly decorated pair of wooden chopsticks, guaranteed to make our meal authentic. Getting the food off the plate and into my mouth was a challenge. But, oh, how much tastier than Chun King from a can!

Then the cookies came. Excitement mounted as we read each fortune while sucking on the sweetness of the broken cookies. During the long drive home, I sat clutching my souvenir chopsticks, wondering if there was any chance my fortune would come true.

Our children do not share the same enthusiasm for Chinese food. When they hear *stir-fry for supper,* their shoulders sag. It doesn't matter if the sun is shining, friends are coming, or an outing is planned; stir-fry dampens the entire day. This, in spite of the years I've spent learning how to throw things in a wok.

It all started when I discovered a show on PBS. The teaser said, "Yan can cook, AND YOU CAN TOO." I watched Yan slice, dice, mix, and throw, and I took meticulous notes on ingredients. Later, I sliced, diced, heated up my frying pan, and started throwing things in. Yan always looked happy. His 15-minute finished product always received applause. My 2-hour version was eaten, but there was no applause.

I guessed that I needed to learn more about the whole procedure. So I set out to get an education, checking out books from the library and experimenting on my family. But the frying pan still produced limp vegetables and sagging shoulders in my kids.

By now my children were old enough to have developed lifelong opinions regarding the foods they ate. They liked the rice. So when I placed a small spoonful of stir-fry on their plates they didn't starve. They just separated out all the stir-fried food and asked for more rice.

Then one day a genuine wok suddenly appeared. My husband brought it home from a garage sale. It was already seasoned to perfection, caked with black from years of use. I was ecstatic. My own wok! My children just shuddered and groaned a two-syllable "Da-ad!"

Stir-fry immediately took on new meaning. My new wok produced intense heat. Nothing could hold me back. That's when Mark brought the fire extinguisher up from the basement. He also realized that the kitchen was not a safe place for our children anymore. Thus, the warning cry was born: "Everyone out of the kitchen! Mom's doing stir-fry!"

My kids each have their favorite episode of my stir-frying failures. They frequently bring these up for a hoot at dinnertime, howling with laughter. I tell myself it is good for their digestion. They especially like the time my wok caught on fire.

That night I had stopped midstream to help Katherine take some medicine. When she spit out the disgusting liquid, I bent down to clean up the floor, not noticing the black cloud forming. When the smoke alarm went off, the rest of the family came running just in time to see the flames erupt. As I charged out of the front door with the smoking wok, I heard one of them hopefully asking, "Does this mean we won't be having stir-fry tonight?"

My education with the wok continues to this day. Hopefully I am getting wiser as I learn more about the process.

Learning and wisdom seem to go hand in hand. In fact, when it comes to getting an education, the Bible makes a point of making wisdom the ultimate goal of learning. "Do not forsake wisdom, and she will protect you; love her and she will watch over you. Wisdom is supreme; therefore get wisdom. Though it cost all you have, get understanding" (Proverbs 4:6,7).

During my years as a student, I never really understood wisdom. I was under the impression that wisdom was directly related to how smart you were or how well you did in school. But this kind of education is not found at a prestigious college or under the watchful eye of a brilliant tutor. Proverbs says, "The LORD gives wisdom, and from his mouth come knowledge and understanding" (Proverbs 2:6). This kind of wise understanding is found in the Word of God. Supreme wisdom is obtained by following God's laws. "The fear of the LORD is the beginning of wisdom; all who follow his precepts have good understanding" (Psalm 111:10).

A king's education

Long ago, a young boy stumbled across this education quite by accident. His father, the king, had been assassinated in his own palace. Little Josiah was only eight years old when he became king. His father and grandfather did evil in the eyes of the Lord and worshiped idols. But little Josiah avoided this influence. Second Kings tells us that this young king "did what was right in the eyes of the LORD and walked in all the ways of his father David" (2 Kings 22:2). "In the eighth year of his reign, while he was still young, he began to seek the God of his father David. In his twelfth year he began to purge Judah and Jerusalem of . . . idols" (2 Chronicles 34:3).

Josiah systematically got rid of the evil influences, altars, and priests of idols. In his search for understanding, Josiah decided to purify the temple. Many previous kings had allowed the temple to fall into a sad state of ruin. So, money was collected, overseers were chosen, and jobs were entrusted to able carpenters and builders. The slow process of restoring the Lord's temple began.

As work proceeded on the temple, the priest made a startling discovery. He found the Book of the Law of the Lord! This included the book of Deuteronomy, which contains the entire Mosaic Law. Faith in God and love towards one's neighbor are at the heart of God's Law.

Picture young King Josiah as the secretary read the words of Moses out loud for the first time. Josiah had spent ten years trying to purify his kingdom as he thought the Lord wanted. Now he was learning about the fear of the Lord. His new understanding showed him how far his kingdom had fallen. He was getting an education that went far beyond purging and purifying. The words hit home: "And now, O Israel, what does the LORD your God ask of you but to fear the LORD your God, to walk in all his ways, to love him, to serve the LORD your God with all your heart and with all your soul, and to observe the LORD's commands and decrees that I am giving you today for your own good?" (Deuteronomy 10:12,13).

Christian education

Unlike Josiah, my childhood was blessed with parents who provided a good education for me. I attended Christian schools for most of my school years, including college. My education centered on God's Word. My teachers taught from this source of wisdom. I worshiped, prayed, and read the Bible with my fellow classmates. I grew up in the rich soil described in the parable of the sower.

My life continued in Christian education even after college. As a teacher, I realized my education was just beginning. Each new student who walked into my classroom was actually a continuing education for me. I studied each child with his or her distinctive needs and abilities. My responsibility to teach went beyond the basics; my teaching touched the souls of my students.

Josiah thought he knew what the Lord wanted, but he needed direction. The Book of the Law provided that direction. In my teaching, I provided the same direction through God's Word. Saint Paul eloquently explains how I viewed my work in the classroom: "My purpose is that they may be encouraged in heart and united in love, so that they have the full riches of complete understanding, in order that they may know the mystery of God, namely, Christ, in whom are hidden all the treasures of wisdom and knowledge" (Colossians 2:2,3).

The full riches of complete understanding should happen on a daily basis in a Christian classroom. Christian education has two words in it. If one part is missing the whole is lacking.

But classrooms—even Christian classrooms—are filled with sinners. Unfortunately there are times when the morning's lessons in God's Word were untaught later in the day. And actions often speak louder than words, even louder than God's Word. And as a result, some children will inevitably suffer.

When a child suffers from the willful meanness of others, school becomes a burden. There is no safe place, except under the watchful eyes of a caring teacher. But this sin of meanness is carried out in secret. And it is especially painful when it affects one of your own children.

Dan did not care for rough-housing. He was interested in learning. But as his education proceeded, he mainly learned how to avoid confrontations. By the time he was nine, he had learned that teachers wouldn't help him, parents couldn't change things, and school was the ultimate test of endurance.

One day, while waiting to pick Dan up after school, I watched our son trudge across the parking lot. My windows were rolled down to let in the beautiful weather. A classmate spied our son halfway to the safety of our car. "Hey! There goes Stupid," he shouted. Several others echoed, "Hey, Stupid!" The words seemed to bounce off our son's shoulders. The parents of the offending boys quietly looked on. The offenders finally stopped when our car door slammed shut.

Dan simply said, "Let's go home."

That day I went home with silent tears and took another look at Christian education. The shelter of this environment had failed our son.

My husband and I had another long conversation. I cried again as we talked about the years of physical and emotional hurt that had followed our son through different schools. And I prayed for wisdom, using this Bible promise as my encouragement: "If any of you lacks wisdom, he should ask God, who gives generously to all without finding fault, and it will be given him" (James 1:5).

As a parent I have made mistakes. There were times when I remained quiet, not wanting to question a teacher's judgment. There were times when I took away privileges at home because Dan wasn't behaving in school. Conferences with teachers brought different advice: "I can't do anything about it unless I see it happen." "He needs to learn how to handle confrontation." And one, repeated often, "I wish just once he'd hit back."

Through all those years we prayed with our son and for our son. We prayed for those who hurt him too. The hardest part was the deep down hurt that comes with the feeling that we were failures as Christian parents. Our son did not want to forgive others.

Proverbs 4:7 says, "Though it cost all you have, get understanding." As parents it was time to provide for that education. But our decision was especially hard because both of us have devoted our lives to Christian education. As teachers, we have been dedicated to our classrooms and students. Still, in spite of all this, we decided to remove our own son from this environment. His home-schooling years began in fifth grade.

Blessed with a difficult decision

Our decision received mixed reactions that ranged from anger to confusion. Some made an effort to correct what, to them, seemed to be an error in judgment. Caring hugs were offered to encourage me with my "willful child." One person insinuated that I should change my career. We had to be especially careful not to project feelings of bitterness or injustice to others in our conversations. Trying to make them understand our need to home-school would only have created hard feelings. So our prayers focused on Dan's immediate needs and our desire to move forward.

As I spent the next several years sitting alongside our son, sharing his education, I grew. I discovered there was real joy to be found in teaching my own child. I lived each day with the words that Josiah read: "Love the LORD your God with all your heart and with all your soul and with all your strength. These commandments that I give you today are to be upon your hearts. Impress them on your children. Talk about them when you sit at home and when you walk along the road, when you lie down and when you get up" (Deuteronomy 6:5-7).

I treasured those mornings we spent studying God's Word together. Dan slowly let go of his past and focused on his worth in God's sight through Christ's redemption. For the first time in his life, the impact of his own forgiveness became relevant. The words of Colossians became personal: "Bear with each other and forgive whatever grievances you may have against one another. Forgive as the Lord forgave you. And over all these virtues put on love, which binds them all together in perfect unity" (Colossians 3:13,14). His self-doubts and fears lessened.

I was forced to brush up on my algebra and history. And I began to see Christian education with new understanding. I learned that the primary responsibility of Christian education remains in the hands of parents, not in the curriculum of schools. Christian education occurs when children are still sitting in laps and holding hands to take walks. Christian education fills every moment and circumstance of the day.

I thank God for both sets of grandparents. As we struggled with our questions and preconceived notions, they supported us with their prayers and encouragement. Their love was such a blessing when we were filled with uncertainty and doubt.

The Lord blessed us with an extra measure of patience in our relationships with those who spoke against us and for the times of butting heads with my own student. We had much for which to be thankful.

I thanked God also for those who gave encouragement without a need to know details, for former teachers who remained supportive, and for his pastor, who instilled in Dan a love and respect for God's Word. And I thanked God for one very special teacher who was a member of the staff of the school that Dan had been attending.

When Dan was in fourth grade, this teacher saw in Dan an individual with unique needs of his own. Instead of trying to make him fit the mold, she provided endless opportunities to learn and make friends. She held him accountable, along with all his classmates, for their actions in the light of God's Word. She brought laughter and love into that classroom. She took chances in her teaching; her flexibility allowed for trying new things. Learning was enjoyable. I cherish that teacher, not just because of the knowledge Dan gained but because she gave him a year he will remember for life.

Continuing education

My education continues in many areas. I gave up trying to home-school when I had to study harder than our son. But as a result of this experience, I became more open as a person. When an educational opportunity arose for our daughter, we hesitated but did not hold her back. She attended a special program in the public school for four years. Her primary learning still took place "in our laps." She studied God's Word along with Dan before climbing onto the school bus. Watching her leave the first day was stressful. I had heard about the evils of public education. But she too was blessed.

Our daughter met many wonderful Christians during her four years attending public school. Contrary to popular opinion, beliefs are not taken for granted there just because the environment is a secular one. As she learned about other people's beliefs, we studied them around our own kitchen table, in the light of God's Word. She became confident to speak up for her Savior—a witness to her classmates. She shared her beliefs about unborn children with the librarian who wore the same tiny pin of gold feet. She met the substitute teacher who always brought his well-worn Bible to read during silent reading time. She learned to treasure her own faith and realized how blessed she was to have a faith firmly established in God's Word.

God blessed Josiah for his commitment and faithfulness. Neither his father before him nor his son after him served the Lord. Josiah was unique, choosing to follow the Lord at a time and in a place in which it was the unusual thing to do. Josiah's education lasted a lifetime. His dedication is held up as an example to those who seek wisdom.

Josiah received quite a tribute in 2 Kings 23:25, "Neither before nor after Josiah was there a king like him who turned to the LORD as he did—with all his heart and with all his soul and with all his strength, in accordance with all the Law of Moses."

I have never given up on the idea of creating the perfect stir-fry meal just because of drooping shoulders, sagging vegetables, or unexpected fires. As a parent I am also still learning. The experiences of my children have strengthened me as a parent and as a teacher. The Lord's blessings were obvious along the way. My faith grew. My relationship with my children grew. And I came to an even greater appreciation for God's wisdom: "Oh, the depth of the riches of the wisdom and knowledge of God! How unsearchable his judgments, and his paths beyond tracing out!" (Romans 11:33). There is always more to learn when it comes to divine wisdom.

One day our youngest announced that she was "retiring from school" and needed me to stay home to home-school her. She didn't get her wish; her needs didn't require it. In fact, she attends the same school where I teach. All three of our children continue their Christian education, first at home and then aided by our church.

The book of Proverbs says: "I guide you in the way of wisdom and lead you along straight paths. When you walk, your steps will not be hampered; when you run, you will not stumble. Hold on to instruction, do not let it go; guard it well, for it is your life" (Proverbs 4:11-13).

CHAPTER NINE

The Competition

We live in a sprawling metropolitan area. Literally hundreds of thousands of people travel our roads, shop in our stores, and live in this small piece of real estate. So the day our daughter saw the announcement "Mother's Day Writing Contest" in the newspaper, she knew it would be a tough competition.

Elizabeth loves to write. Ever since she was two years old, she has enjoyed the effects of pencil on paper. Encouraged in the past by her third grade teacher, she learned how to communicate her thoughts, feelings, and imaginations through the written word. She was eager to capture others in her world of words. "Tell us why your mom is the best mom in the world" was the ad's challenge.

Elizabeth also loves competition. Just the word *contest* can capture her attention. This time the competition came with an enticing prize dangling like raw meat above a trap. "First Place Prize: A $200.00 gift certificate at the Mall, lunch at the Cliff House Restaurant overlooking Puget Sound, 2 free tickets to Wildwaves, and a certificate to pamper your mom at a local spa."

She grabbed paper and pencil and disappeared, ignoring her free weekend afternoon. Two hours later, she emerged, handed me a paper and queried, "What do you think?" I read her words praising me for my baking and my beauty.

Looking up at her beaming face, I knew honesty was needed. Gently I guided her. "If you really want to write something that will win, you will have to grab their attention."

"Yes, but you don't do anything that grabs attention."

I smiled. "Well then, you'll have to look for something unique. Everyone writes things like, 'I love my mom because she's so nice.' Make other people see me through your words."

She looked at me, her countenance darkening. "You don't like it."

"I do like it, but I know you can do better. Take some time to let your thoughts settle."

Several days later she appeared with a new paper. "I did what you said." But this time her optimism was tempered with caution.

I read her careful sentences with colorful adjectives. It was well written for a sixth grader. She sensed my hedging and asked, "Do you think I will win?"

My honesty was not well received.

"But I worked on it for days!" she countered.

I suggested that she ask her teacher for advice.

At the end of the week, she quietly handed me three pages of writing. "I talked to my teacher, and she said the same thing you did. So I started over."

I took her writing and read about myself. Her words captured me . . . and exposed me. I read about my quirks, my beliefs, and my influences through the eyes of my daughter. This time when I finished reading, she was smiling. She didn't have to ask; she knew. We went through the simple editing process. She recopied and mailed it in.

Then the competition took on a new meaning.

Never before had my daughter had that much money to spend in one place. Her gift certificates were good for one year, compounding her dilemma. She spent her moments with the sale ads, hungry with a young teen's *wants*. She carefully priced and planned. Months later she sighed with resignation as she spent her last certificate.

"I guess $200.00 really isn't that much, is it, Mom?" I looked at my daughter and remembered when I had made the same discovery. I reminded her that it was $200.00 more than she had had before winning the contest.

A parallel from Scripture

A picture from Genesis comes to my mind when I think of life's pursuits. I see it from above, like looking down from a distant hilltop. Two processions move slowly toward each other. The hot, dusty air is tense, as if a battle will unfold before my eyes. The group coming from the southwest numbers four hundred men. The opposing group comes in waves, a mixture of adults, children, and animals. The leaders of the two groups are brothers, Jacob and Esau by name. Jacob, the leader of the mixed group, walks with a noticeable limp. Not long ago he wrestled with the Son of God, winning for himself a blessing. The limp was a permanent reminder that just wrestling with God is already a blessing of the highest order. When the two groups finally meet, the brothers embrace, melting away years of bitterness. Waves of exuberant people from both sides gather around the two men. Jacob and Esau had made a complete about-face.

How different the picture had been 20 years earlier when Jacob fled from his brother. The road that stretched before Jacob lay in darkness. During that first long night, with a stone for his pillow and miles from the comforts of his home and family, he had slept. Fitfully. But his heavenly dream had brought this promise: "I am with you and will watch over you wherever you go, and I will bring you back to this land. I will not leave you until I have done what I have promised you." That promise brought Jacob peace.

It was strange to read in Elizabeth's essay: "My mom values many things. She values our family life. We always eat dinner together, sharing stories from our day. My mom finds traditions very important. Holidays and birthdays are days for special things." I was proud of her writing accomplishment but felt oddly uneasy about her subject. Her words generated a good deal of soul searching, as I began to wonder if I was living up to the image she portrayed.

I read on: "My mom is a very busy person. She directs the choir at church and also takes her turn playing the organ for services. She teaches art at Evergreen Lutheran High School and teaches piano too. She also drives my siblings and me wherever we need to go, cooks, and cleans. Even though her life is hectic and full of things, she enjoys it and takes it as a challenge."

Busy! Hectic! Challenging! Her words so aptly described my days that it was uncanny. How I longed for the simplicity described in 1 Thessalonians chapter 4! "Make it your ambition to lead a quiet life, to mind your own business and to work with your hands, just as we told you, so that your daily life may win the respect of outsiders and so that you will not be dependent on anybody."

Jacob's journey came to a place where he could stop and rest. Working for his uncle, he had plenty of time to reminisce about his past. He fell in love, married, and worked with his hands. Sin was still part of the picture. But under the Lord's continued guidance, Jacob grew as a provider, a husband, a father, and a child of God.

I wondered if that was where I was in life? Stopping and resting? Or was I at a turning point in life, at a transition?

After staying home with our children for many years, I was now bringing in a regular paycheck. At times I felt uneasy about the change, as though I was leaving behind my role as a Christian wife and mother to pursue more selfish ambitions. I have seen the perceived "need for money" in other families coincide with an increase in their level of luxury. Now I was beginning to wonder if the same thing was happening to me. Owning a small home, buying more convenient groceries instead of "laying up" the harvests from my garden, paying for more gas, more lessons, more basketball shoes . . . Our standard of living was certainly rising. Paul warned young Timothy: "Some people, eager for money, have wandered from the faith and pierced themselves with many griefs" (1 Timothy 6:10). I considered the possibility that I was falling into that trap, enjoying the conveniences of money. Or were those so-called conveniences necessary so that I could continue to teach? And wasn't my teaching also another way of serving my God with the gifts and abilities he had given me?

Our struggles are good. From them we learn that only God can bring them to a resolution that is in keeping with his will. The tension between working and staying home with my children brought growth and the many blessings that come with revisiting God's will for our lives. Paul was right when he wrote, "It is God who works in you to will and to act according to his good purpose" (Philippians 2:13). The struggle meant that God was still working on me, perfecting me, shaping me according to his good purpose.

The Lord blessed Jacob just as he had promised. His family grew, and so did his possessions. By the time Jacob was ready to return home and face his brother, he was a wealthy man. It was God's purpose to fulfill the promises made to Jacob's father and grandfather through Jacob and his offspring. The Lord had secured the future for Jacob and his children's children.

The questions Christians may have about the goals they pursue in life need to focus on God's will. Whatever our goals may be, we need to pursue them as a daily walk with the Lord.

The pitfalls of celebrity

Elizabeth's experience with the competition did not end when she cashed in her last coupon. Our picture graced the front page of a section of our local newspaper. Easily recognized, we were now approached in public. "Aren't you the ones in the paper?" people would ask. Conversations followed; total strangers talked with me about their approach to motherhood. The problem was that we were not always the living examples of what Elizabeth's essay professed.

One shopping trip, in particular, was memorable. Teenage desire collided head-on with motherly sensibility. She huffed. I puffed. We stood, rigid, in silent face-to-face combat in the middle of the socks section of a department store. The air crackled with raw emotion. Then another smiling face appeared. "Excuse me, but aren't you the ones in the newspaper?"

We didn't do too well with the words from Colossians that day: "Be wise in the way you act toward outsiders; make the most of every opportunity. Let your conversation be always full of grace, seasoned with salt, so that you may know how to answer everyone" (Colossians 4:5,6). It is very difficult to stop huffing and puffing for the sake of appearances and change gears instantaneously.

You'd think we would all learn our lessons. Jacob apparently didn't. The victim of favoritism in his own growing-up years, Jacob turned around and dealt the same cards to his own sons. Even my young students are able to see where Jacob failed. His sins were obvious. The beauty of Jacob's story is not to be found in the ambitions of a young entrepreneur, or an energetic father, or a strategic planner. The beauty of his life lies in the keeper of the promises—the One who forgives—the One who heals. He who looks down with perfect love, guiding, directing, watching, challenging, brought blessing upon blessing into Jacob's life, even as the wrestling match continued.

The same almighty God is ever present in my life and in the life of my competitive daughter. He is the same yesterday, today, and forever. We'll make mistakes. But with Christ at the center of our lives, our decisions will be blessed. We don't have to flounder around in a quandary, wondering if we have filled "a woman's place" or carried out "the perfect role." Besides, I will be too busy competing for *the prize,* right alongside my daughter. "Forgetting what is behind and straining toward what is ahead, I press on toward the goal to win the prize for which God has called me heavenward in Christ Jesus" (Philippians 3:13,14).

CHAPTER TEN

Contentment

We had a dog once. A long while ago. What a dog she was! She wasn't planned. She just happened into our lives. One hot, summer day she found us.

After a summer school class in New Ulm, Minnesota, Mark and I drove a classmate to her home on a small Minnesota farm. As we stopped in her driveway, a bundle of pups erupted from a nearby shed, romping around our car. As we got out to stretch our legs, the puppies bounded past us, avoiding our efforts to pet them. We tried to continue our conversation only to be interrupted by a movement alongside the house. Out from the bushes stepped the youngest pup, using only three legs. She seemed frail, beautiful, and in great need. Her eyes drooped in sadness as she avoided the playfulness of her siblings. Instead, with the elegance of a James Herriot character, she limped over to my husband and softly, gently, licked his hand. They bonded.

Hannah was part of our family for 15 years. Her hip socket, injured in an accident, eventually healed. She learned to run, leap for Frisbees, and herd our cats, since we had no sheep. She was a gentle, caring dog—a special playmate to each of our children as they learned to walk, give orders, and share toys. She loved to play with them. But her heart belonged to Mark.

When Mark was home, she was always nearby. When he went for walks, she happily tagged along. Our camping trips and vacations included Hannah. She rode in the front seat of the car so she could keep an eye on Mark. She followed Mark everywhere, sharing his rambunctious times and his quiet times. In fact, it could be said she mirrored his moods, communicating her understanding with her eyes. Every night she would settle down by his bedside and let out a deep sigh before falling asleep. With Mark nearby, she was totally content.

An elusive treasure

Contentment. Without it life does not have calm. True happiness is interwoven with the fibers of contentment. All people seek to own it; yet, it eludes many. Contentment cannot be purchased or given as a gift. It cannot be earned through years of service. It is not found in a cup of tea, a fragrant candle, or a perfect exercise. It is not connected to who I am or what I have.

When I was very young I didn't think about contentment. It wasn't until responsibilities and desires started complicating my life that I noticed that I was not always content.

I started to seek contentment. During my high school years I thought if I had the right clothes, acceptance among my peers, or a personality that was popular, I would surely be content. In Bible words, "When I was a child, I talked like a child, I thought like a child, I reasoned like a child" (1 Corinthians 13:11).

When I reached college and met my future spouse, I thought that contentment would be found in our future home together. We would have a wonderful house, children, and two cats in the yard. I could hardly wait for married bliss. Surely that would fill my life with genuine contentment.

The married bliss came, but contentment was still elusive.

During the childless years, I was sure that babies were the source of contentment. Wrong again! But it was about this time that I started to grasp the pattern. With each new direction my life took, each planned step I took down my path, contentment remained one step ahead of me. I could never quite reach it.

Now, years later, I have finally caught up with that elusive bend in the road where contentment hides. But what I have discovered is quite different from what I had imagined. You see, it's not a matter of catching up with anything. It's simply a matter of understanding one truth: "Godliness with contentment is great gain" (1 Timothy 6:6).

Unlocking the mystery

One day, on a quiet hillside in Galilee, Jesus taught his followers about this great, elusive *gain* that everyone strives to have. Sitting on a rock, he spoke to his disciples about their life in this world as children of God. That life holds the secrets of a contentment that is at once profound as well as lasting.

"Do not store up for yourselves treasures on earth, where moth and rust destroy, and where thieves break in and steal," he said. "But store up for yourselves treasures in heaven, where moth and rust do not destroy, and where thieves do not break in and steal. For where your treasure is, there your heart will be also" (Matthew 6:19-21).

It took my heart many years to realize I was so blessed. My life is filled with treasures. They are spiritual in nature, but hardly abstract. I still don't keep up with the latest fashions or have the house of my dreams. It may seem odd, but I don't even desire them anymore. My desires have changed. I believe what the psalmist wrote, "Delight yourself in the LORD and he will give you the desires of your heart" (Psalm 37:4).

Knowing *what to desire* is the best-kept secret of the ages. Therein lies the key.

God's creation is one of my treasures. I have always enjoyed the beautiful glow of the dawning sky, the fresh vibrant colors of a garden's new growth, the radiating shades and hues of a flowerbed. My husband has helped expand my appreciation for the wonders of life on earth. He has taught me to see and hear the nature that surrounds us—the birds of the air, the wildflowers, the never-ending stars that grace our night skies, and the infinite variety of bugs that creep and crawl through our lives, mostly unnoticed.

I can still remember the first time I heard the distinctive song of an indigo bunting. Walking in the direction of the song, my husband and I were rewarded with an incredible sight. In the dappled sunshine of the new spring growth, sat a male bunting. His blue glow was brilliant in comparison to his surroundings—a perfectly beautiful species in God's endless spectacle. We stared, silently soaking in the sight and the sound as he sang his territorial song. Such treasures are rare.

During another walk in early summer, when the forest floor had grown as tall as my knees, I heard a soft clucking sound. Not knowing what it was, I froze. Nothing. Then I took another careful step, my senses alert. Almost magically a wild turkey materialized from the undergrowth just a few feet away. Sensing her exposure, she again made the soft clucking sound, and turkey chicks suddenly began scampering across my shoes, their downy bodies bumping into one another as they ran straight to their mother. I didn't even get a chance to count them before they disappeared into the shadows of the forest.

These times are more than simple treasures. They are moments when nature shows me the greatness of God's power—reminders that he is in charge and there is nothing under the sun to worry about. Jesus said it like this: "Therefore I tell you, do not worry about your life, what you will eat or drink; or about your body, what you will wear. Is not life more important than food, and the body more important than clothes? Look at the birds of the air; they do not sow or reap or store away in barns, and yet your heavenly Father feeds them. Are you not much more valuable than they? Who of you by worrying can add a single hour to his life?" (Matthew 6:25-27).

A new treasure

And yet, I worry. Even with all of the promises in Scripture, all the lessons taught in nature, and all the blessings I've experienced in my life, I still worry. It's a nagging, constant destroyer that chips away at contentment. And it can bring a host of evil companions: discontent, greed, jealousy, false pride. These feed on one another, compounding the worry. It can consume a person, so that even when you go to God to "ask, seek, and knock," worry's talons are hard to loosen.

When we moved to southern California, I worried. Gone were the comfortable home, the woods, the parks with songbirds, cross-country skiing, autumn colors, and spring's magical rebirth. They were replaced with concrete, asphalt, the noise of an airport, traffic, and trains. Everything seemed hot, dusty, and dirty. And expensive! We needed to find a place to live in this concrete jungle. Buying a home was out of the question, and no clean apartment would allow two cats and a dog. But Jesus said, "Who of you by worrying can add a single hour to his life?"

Some might call it a coincidence. Not me. I have harvested handfuls from the Lord too often to consider it pure luck. The day before our belongings arrived in a U-Haul truck, we heard about an empty condo. The owners were hesitant to rent to us because of our dog Hannah. But we loaded our suitcases and pets into the car and went to meet our prospective landlords anyway.

They lived in the hills overlooking our concrete valley. And, they had a little girl. When we arrived at their beautiful home, Hannah hopped out of the car, timidly walked up to their daughter, dropped her ball, and gently licked the little girl's hand. Then she looked up into the little girl's face with her pleading eyes. Hannah got a hug. We got the condo.

But on that warm summer day, I had no idea of the other blessings still in store for us. I only knew that we were ready to begin the Lord's work in a new place. Our condo, part of a four-unit building complete with four bachelors and their large dog living above us, would soon feel like home. My heart still missed the wide-open yard, the beautiful trees, and the calm of Michigan. So I filled our tiny back porch with flowerpots. We put up a hummingbird feeder. As we sat at our table, God's creation came to us. (Southern California has quite a variety of those amazing hummers, small miracles of aerial wonder.) Our lives were ripe with blessings—new experiences, new Christian friends, and the wonderful blessing of a baby. Looking back, I believe this was the beginning of contentment.

Simple, yet sufficient

Jesus continued his hillside teaching:

And why do you worry about clothes? See how the lilies of the field grow. They do not labor or spin. Yet I tell you that not even Solomon in all his splendor was dressed like one of these. If that is how God clothes the grass of the field, which is here today and tomorrow is thrown into the fire, will he not much more clothe you, O you of little faith? So do not worry, saying, "What shall we eat?" or "What shall we drink?" or "What shall we wear?" For the pagans run after all these things, and your heavenly Father knows that you need them. But seek first his kingdom and his righteousness, and all these things will be given to you as well.

As our needs rose, so did our dependency on God. We turned to the Lord daily in his Word. Our faith grew. I learned that no matter how hard I lean on God, he always holds me up. As I learned these lessons, I began to store up new treasures that were more closely connected to heaven than to earth. God's words to a beleaguered Saint Paul took on new meaning: "My grace is sufficient for you, for my power is made perfect in [your] weakness" (2 Corinthians 12:9). It helped me see that the things Jesus promised in Matthew chapter 6 will exceed and transcend earthly needs.

It seems almost illogical to be content with little when surrounded by a society that thrives on extravagant desires and disposable belongings. I am convinced that my riches exceeded those of the mansion owners who lived only a few blocks away. You can't put a price on a faithful marriage, for instance. And those moments of laughter at our supper table . . . how do you put a price tag on that?

The secret of deep contentment

I believe that true contentment comes only through the eyes of faith. Faith brings an understanding of peace with God. That peace spills over into every other area in life.

My riches are found in Jesus, my Savior. He has bought me, paid for my life with his own blood. I am his. Not only me, but those whom I love, as well. All the blessings God has promised are ours, as free as the gift of salvation. The riches of Jesus' grace, his death, and the resurrection to life everlasting are the secret to a contentment that penetrates deep into one's soul. Paul expressed it this way: "I have learned to be content whatever the circumstances. I know what it is to be in need, and I know what it is to have plenty. I have learned the secret of being content in any and every situation, whether well fed or hungry, whether living in plenty or in want. I can do everything through him who gives me strength" (Philippians 4:11-13).

In our concrete backyard, a small square was cut out of the sidewalk. A tree grew in this small patch of dirt. To that small tree God sent a pair of hummingbirds to build their nest and raise their young. This nest was about the size of a baby's palm; its eggs half as big as my little fingernail. So frail! Yet, protected. Not only by the faithful parents, but by the almighty Creator who cares for each one. That little nest was perched in the tree right outside the window by my baby's crib. I could not help but think of the words: "O you of little faith, . . . are you not much more valuable than they?"

There, in that tiny apartment, in a little corner of southern California, we were frail, yet protected. Weak, yet strong in God's grace. Every earthly need was richly, lovingly provided. We had food, clothing, and more than enough baby items. Christian friends opened up their hands and their hearts. Our little apartment was a safe haven, protected from the troubles of the world around us.

That's the secret. Contentment is really not so elusive after all. The words of Psalm 37 tell the whole story: "Trust in the LORD and do good; dwell in the land and enjoy safe pasture. Delight yourself in the LORD and he will give you the desires of your heart. Commit your way to the LORD; trust in him and he will do this: He will make your righteousness shine like the dawn, the justice of your cause like the noonday sun. Be still before the LORD and wait patiently for him."

My contentment still surprises me. When I least expect it, I am overwhelmed with gratitude for my blessings. We work, love, laugh, and play in the joy of being redeemed, forgiven children of God. This contentment leaves a delicious sense of security.

And then there is me, a woman of God. I am content with my life. I have been redeemed. My faith puts everything else into perspective. All my tasks, ambitions, and joys revolve around that faith. Such contentment gives me the boldness to talk to my Creator as my dear Father. He handles all my cares, my fears, and my needs. I live in the certainty of my future—a place in God's eternal kingdom. And all of this comes free—a gift from a gracious God.

To his fellow Christians living in Ephesus, Paul once wrote, "I pray that you, being rooted and established in love, may have power . . . to grasp how wide and long and high and deep is the love of Christ" (Ephesians 3:17,18). It is a prayer I often pray for myself. In the simple blessings that come with finding contentment in his love, those prayers are answered.

CHAPTER ELEVEN

To Grow Old Beautifully

We had been warned. The friendly advice came in the form of a question: Who would want to live in Seattle, where your toothbrush never dries out? But we moved anyway.

It truly does rain nine months out of the year in Seattle. Many visitors are surprised by the cold that accompanies the damp. It's bone chilling to flatlanders.

Call me wimpy, but I've come to love this corner of the world. I've acclimated to the wet toothbrush. I enjoy the overcast skies. I'm past the days of worrying about tan lines or wet hair anyway. On the rare sunny days when God permits a view of our beautiful mountain, I squint and quickly pull out my sunglasses. I wear socks with my sandals, sweatshirts with my shorts, and I don't carry an umbrella. After all, it is only water.

But, as in any place, there are a few things I don't appreciate. Three immediately come to mind: slimy slugs, dirty carpet inside the front door, and mold. I know how to handle the giant slugs. (Don't ask.) I can recommend a great carpet cleaner. But the mold finally got the upper hand in our house.

My husband prefers a good book, jazz on the radio, and a quiet afternoon. So the prospect of tackling the mold behind the tiles in our bathroom didn't excite him in the least. But once he gets started, he doesn't like to be interrupted. So when Mark started "The Bathroom Wall" project, the rest of us cleared out, leaving him all the space that he needed.

He was well into his third day of kneeling in the tub when the kitchen faucet broke. It just gave out. Within moments water was coming out in a nonstop heavy stream, no little drip-drop warning. Mark had to be called off the tub-'n'-tile project to tackle the trickle.

I knew it was time for me to do something constructive. But I don't know anything about faucets and there is only room enough for one person under our sink. So I began to clean the carpet by the front door. Mark was still under the sink, studying the faucet, when I was finally ready to vacuum the clean, dry carpet. When I turned on the vacuum, a putrid odor filled the air. The motor was melting the recently replaced belt. I shut it off and glanced at the bottom half of Mark protruding from the uncomfortable spot underneath the sink. "Dear . . . ?" I timidly told his feet, "I think the vacuum cleaner just died."

When things get old, they wear out. Owning a house brings this fact into sharp focus. There's no way to avoid it. Unfortunately, the same thing is happening to my body.

A few years ago I took up jogging in an attempt to counter some of the aging. I gave that up the day I became airborne from catching my shoe on the edge of the driveway. I don't like that many scabs. Now I use the *machine* in our garage—the one affectionately known as the Hamster Wheel. I am also trying out those lotion samples that guarantee my "wrinkles will disappear." I pay attention to nutrition and vitamins and have cut back on some of my favorite foods. Just some of them, though. Deep down I realize that none of these attempts will really slow the aging process.

What is it about growing old that brings denial and fear?

Aging with beauty

The Bible does not speak of old age as something to fear. Proverbs 16:31 says, "Gray hair is a crown of splendor." The Bible also gives a glimpse of some elderly God-fearing women. Luke introduces us to a prophetess named Anna. In chapter 2 he tells us, "She never left the temple but worshiped night and day, fasting and praying."

Anna aged beautifully. She stayed close to the Lord. I picture her as white haired and slightly bent with age. Whenever she smiles her wrinkles accentuate the joy she carries inside. She is a willing, gentle, caring-grandma type, available for any service to anyone who comes into the temple.

I once met a woman like Anna. Emma belonged to our church in Wisconsin. She was a widow. Her own family did not come to our church, but they willingly gave her rides whenever she needed one. She was always helping. I was surprised when we celebrated her 80th birthday.

Emma taught our largest Sunday school class—the youngest ones. She always had a special measure of patience for this age group. Our Sunday school was supposed to start at age 4, but there were many 3-year-olds who learned about Jesus at Emma's feet. When my own daughter was one of those "too soon" students, I started to notice Emma's exceptional qualities.

One Sunday I noticed Emma standing up a little slower than usual. I remarked, "These kids sure do have a lot of energy! How do you keep up with them?"

Emma just smiled. "Oh, it's not hard. They are so much fun, so eager to learn. I love teaching them about God's Word. I never get tired of that."

At that time in my life, I was an exhausted preschool teacher. Keeping up with my own three-year-old required extra calories. I sensed that Emma was embarrassed by the praise. She simply wanted to serve God in any way she was able. I thanked her anyway.

In the years I knew Emma, I don't think I ever heard a single complaint. Her conversation was always more inclined toward the business of building others up. She encouraged even as she witnessed.

Transcending age

In my heart I have a list of women who have influenced my life. As I grow older, my list grows. Like Emma, these women would probably be embarrassed to receive any recognition. I'm sure that I am not the only person with a list like this. These are women who willingly serve their Lord by filling needs in their churches. Their work is done quietly, efficiently, and usually without notice. It becomes expected because of their faithfulness. Much of the work is service done in humility. The needs—whether scrubbing floors, stitching banners, weeding flowerbeds, or bringing in baked goods—aren't scrutinized for value. These women smile as they serve. Their only reward is the joy that such efforts bring to them. They openly praise God in their conversations. The words of Psalm 71 describe what is surely in the hearts of such faithful women: "I will come and proclaim your mighty acts, O Sovereign LORD; I will proclaim your right-eousness, yours alone. Since my youth, O God, you have taught me, and to this day I declare your marvelous deeds. Even when I am old and gray, do not forsake me, O God, till I declare your power to the next generation, your might to all who are to come."

The prophetess Anna must have been like that. Luke recorded the events of the day our infant Savior was brought to the temple. Anna met Joseph and Mary. "Coming up to them at that very moment, she gave thanks to God and spoke about the child to all who were looking forward to the redemption of Jerusalem" (Luke 2:38).

I would like to be like Anna. She went about her work with-out thoughts of self, even with her aging body. She didn't waste energy on worry. She saw what needed to be done, and she served by doing. In both her words and her actions, she wit-nessed to others, telling them about this remarkable child who had come to fulfill the prophecies of old.

I try to emulate these women of God who encourage and build up as they serve. I want the kind of joy they have in spreading the good news of Jesus. But all too often I hear myself complain. I question the task that needs doing or the people I work with. I remind myself that I am tired. I put off what simply needs doing.

The Bible teaches how to become like Anna. The women on my heart list have found this truth as well: "The mind controlled by the Spirit is life and peace" (Romans 8:6). That is the reason for their joyful willingness. "Those who live in accordance with the Spirit have their minds set on what the Spirit desires" (verse 5).

Paul echoed that same thought in the fifth chapter of his letter to the Christians in Galatia, only in terms that reject a life of sin: "Live by the Spirit, and you will not gratify the desires of the sinful nature. For the sinful nature desires what is contrary to the Spirit, and the Spirit what is contrary to the sinful nature."

Living by the Spirit

I think it is difficult to be a person who lives by the Spirit. Difficult, but not impossible. Recall the comments that our daughter Katherine made about her friends all wanting to be like fashion models. Remember the struggle that Elizabeth went through with her shopping spree experience.

The struggle to be a God-fearing woman begins early. Satan's cunning makes good use of his understanding of human growth and development: young minds learn the most. If Satan can plant a seed when our daughters are young, there's a chance that it will sprout as they mature. That is one reason I stayed home with our young children. I wanted to be in control of their environment. It is one of the reasons I still watch carefully as new influences filter into their young lives. I can't control their environment as I could before, but I can be available for all those teachable moments that come from all directions.

Today, beautiful, healthy, successful women portray Satan's seeds of "choice" and "rights." The seeds of logic slip into the cracks of our Bible foundation as we struggle with heavy ideas like embryonic transplants and stem cell research. We have gone way beyond the topics of abortion and premarital sex. The still, small voice of our God sometimes seems lost in the turmoil and hype. I look at our daughters and wonder, "What will it be like when . . ."

The truth remains: God was, is, and always will be present in that still, small voice that guides us through life. And he promises to make us fruitful when we follow his guidance. That's good news! "The fruit of the Spirit is love, joy, peace, patience, kindness, goodness, faithfulness, gentleness and self-control. Against such things there is no law. Those who belong to Christ Jesus have crucified the sinful nature with its passions and desires. Since we live by the Spirit, let us keep in step with the Spirit!" (Galatians 5:22-25).

These fruits of faith are the marks of mature, God-fearing people. To worry about our daughters' futures would be a waste of my time. God has promised he will be there for them just as he has always been there for me. "For I know the plans I have for you . . . plans to prosper you and not to harm you, plans to give you hope and a future. Then you will call upon me and come and pray to me, and I will listen to you. You will seek me and find me when you seek me with all your heart. I will be found by you" (Jeremiah 29:11-14).

The fruits of the Spirit can be found in no other place. Just saying "Today I am going to be more patient and kind!" is like using antiwrinkle cream to avoid aging. The growing comes from God's Spirit. His Spirit works through the Word. That is where we come to know God. That is where we see his plan for us. And that is where we go to know what his will is for our lives of service. "Be very careful, then, how you live—not as unwise but as wise, making the most of every opportunity, because the days are evil. Therefore do not be foolish, but understand what the Lord's will is" (Ephesians 5:15-17).

A life of service

I attended a conference not long ago at which a group of Christian women were discussing the role of women in the church. Many were frustrated. They felt their hands were tied when their hearts wanted to serve. Emotions in the room grew hot as the women fed on one another's frustrations. They did not leave the discussion that day with joy in their hearts or praise on their lips.

I believe there is an answer to their frustrations. I often pray: "Open my eyes to see those in my day who need encouragement. Open my eyes to see ways I can serve today." I think that some days I walk through the daylight hours blind to those in need all around me.

I believe there are situations in which God's capable women are held back. But I also see many times when there is work that needs doing and few hands for serving.

Our children offer me daily opportunities to practice serving joyfully. These days they are perfecting the art of making excuses. Here's how it works:

"Katherine, will you please come and set the table?"

"Huh? What did you say, Mom? I was reading. By the way . . . where's Elizabeth?"

"I asked you to come and set the table. Elizabeth is working on the computer."

"Oh, [pause] don't you remember I did it last night? Isn't it Elizabeth's turn? I'm not at the end of my chapter yet. Isn't reading better for you than computers anyway?"

From the distance a voice answers, "I heard that! Don't argue with Mom, Katherine. Besides, I can't come now. I finally got on. Dan's been hogging the computer all afternoon."

My exasperating experts! I consider a variety of responses. The voice of authority, for one: "Young lady, I told you twice. Get out here right now!" Sarcasm might make the point: "Yes, dear. Reading is so important. Stay there and let me bring you supper." The heat of the stove, and the frustrations of the day, could produce an unwise choice. Paul wrote, "I have the desire to do what is good, but I cannot carry it out. So, I find this law at work: When I want to do good, evil is right there with me" (Romans 7:18,21). Hopefully, the Anna in me will speak instead: "That's okay. I can handle it. You can help me after supper."

I believe that an unselfish attitude, tempered with love and a joyful heart, attracts the attention of those who love you. Quietness can sometimes be louder than words.

I have another favorite part of Scripture that I use in my daily quest to age beautifully. These words come from Paul's letter to the Philippians; I have them printed and taped near all my workspaces around the house:

> Rejoice in the Lord always. I will say it again: Rejoice! Let your gentleness be evident to all. The Lord is near. Do not be anxious about anything, but in everything, by prayer and petition, with thanksgiving, present your requests to God. And the peace of God, which transcends all understanding, will guard your hearts and your minds in Christ Jesus.
>
> Finally . . . whatever is true, whatever is noble, whatever is right, whatever is pure, whatever is lovely, whatever is admirable—if anything is excellent or praiseworthy—think about such things. Whatever you have learned or received or heard from me, or seen in me—put it into practice. And the God of peace will be with you. (Philippians 4:4-9)

Maybe I should tape those words under the sink too.

Our new faucet doesn't trickle, or even drip, when it is turned off. The bathroom tiles turned out to be quite a learning experience. Our new vacuum cleaner works great. The very next morning when Mark unlocked our front door to leave for work, he turned the knob, but the door stayed shut. The deadbolt was dead. He didn't say a word, just turned and grinned. He learned a long time ago that the Lord has a sense of humor. "In his heart a man plans his course, but the LORD determines his steps" (Proverbs 16:9).

Sometimes I wish I could plan the future for my children, but I know the Lord's vision stretches far beyond mine. Even in my middle age, I know my wisdom is lacking. So I consider women like Anna and continue to trust the wisdom of God's ways.

Blessed is the man who finds wisdom,
    the man who gains understanding,
for she is more profitable than silver
    and yields better returns than gold.
She is more precious than rubies;
    nothing you desire can compare with her.
Long life is in her right hand;
    in her left hand are riches and honor.
Her ways are pleasant ways,
    and all her paths are peace.
She is a tree of life to those who embrace her;
    those who lay hold of her will be blessed.
                    (Proverbs 3:13-18)

CHAPTER TWELVE

A Comfortable, Old Sweater

As my morning shower washed off the dull leftovers of sleep, the possibilities of the new day seemed endless. I had the whole day before me. No errands to run, deadlines to meet, or meetings to attend. With the psalmist, I thought, "This is the day the LORD has made; let us rejoice and be glad in it" (Psalm 118:24).

Refreshed, I put on my comfortable, old sweater. It's part of my being home . . . of my being me. I don't remember where it came from, but it has been my comfortable, old sweater for a long time. Two buttons are missing, and the elbows have been stretched to extra sizes. My sweater does not flatter me; it comforts me. Putting on this sweater seems to reinforce my feelings of contentment and project the endless possibilities life has to offer.

I once thought the old sweater was a reflection on our income bracket. A down-to-the-matching-jewelry mother I am not. But neither am I a dumpy stay-at-home mom who goes around in sweaters with buttons missing. I am organized and professional where and when I need to be. When someone asks me who I am, I don't pull out a business card; I smile, instead, and say, "Hello. My name is Rachel, and I am a mom."

I guess who I am is a rather complex subject. The image of a ragged housewife or a harried teacher dissolves into the glorious image of a redeemed, forgiven woman of God. That image is not a matter of pride or accomplishment. It is a gift.

This perfect image comes from the giver of all my gifts; he is the author of my life. It was he who set me apart to be the wife of the bird-watcher; the mother of the long-legged talker, the enchanting ever-evolving teenager, and the mindful musician. The Lord is the one who weaves together my interests in writing, teaching, and music, who delights me with cats, cooking, and colors. He has crafted me to fit perfectly into his plan for a life of service among family and friends.

Making plans

Today, wearing my comfortable, old sweater, I contemplate painting. A new watercolor composition takes shape in my mind. There is much to do before I can apply paint to paper.

Watercolor paper needs to be stretched. It is unforgiving. You can't change your mind and erase great quantities of pencil or paint. It requires gentleness. Even repeated brush strokes can take the life right out of a painting. A watercolor composition takes plenty of forethought and then needs to be executed rapidly. Most of the real work is finished by the time I pick up my brush and load it with color.

I enjoy each step of this process. The ideas come together in my head. Since I am not good at making things up, I often set up my compositions by taking photos, studying them, and sketching out the possibilities. When I have a complete idea in my head (including the size, color, and light variations), I lightly draw my idea on the delicate watercolor paper, planning the progression of each wash. Then I soak the paper, roll it out, and staple it to a board. Only then am I ready to begin painting.

My life resembles a watercolor painting. It has been preplanned. The complex mixture of *who I am* was established before God "knit me together in my mother's womb" (Psalm 139:13). The work of my redemption was accomplished before I took my first steps. I cannot comprehend the vastness of this God who knew me before time began. I only know that he gently sketched me into this moment in time. Then he stretched me to become the woman that I am and colored my life with the blessings that he desired to give. He prepared in advance the work for me to do. "All the days ordained for me were written in [his] book before one of them came to be" (verse 16).

Removing stains

Sometimes, as I paint, my careful planning does not pan out. Sometimes the paper dries too fast. Then the unforgiving qualities of watercolors do not allow me to go over the painting with fresh paint. Often there are interruptions, like doorbells ringing, schedules demanding, or dear children pleading "Mo-om." But the most unplanned, unwelcomed interruption that I have ever experienced was Chuck.

I was excited about this particular painting because all my preplanning was falling into place. My daughters, wearing white summer dresses, were pretending to have a tea party on a quilt in our backyard. I was taking photos as they poured cool lemonade from a white porcelain teapot.

That's when Chuck walked into the picture. He was an orange tabby that came with the neighborhood. He sat front and center, gazing defiantly into the camera. We never argued with Chuck, not even when he decided to adopt us.

The painting of Chuck's tea party was progressing well. This time, the composition focused attention just where I had planned it. The colors provided the feelings one associates with a warm, sunny day, a desirable effect for this part of the country. And I could almost taste that refreshing lemonade.

Unfortunately, I was interrupted with one of those "Mo-om!" calls. I left my painting, carefully setting my brush and palette aside before I left the room. Chuck was sleeping on the chair next to the art table.

When I returned, I was shocked to find dark crimson stains on the carpet leading into the hallway. I followed the stains back to their origin—a wet puddle of paint in the corner of my palette. It was a color I rarely use.

Alizarin crimson is intense. It cannot be erased from watercolor paper because of its staining qualities. It also stains well on carpet, white windowsills, bedspreads, and walls. Chuck had, no doubt, enjoyed the cool sensation as he walked across my palette and loaded up his paws with color.

The carpet demanded my attention first. I quickly sprayed water on it and used a towel to soak up as much color as possible. Next, I captured the peaceful painter, who was sitting on yet another white windowsill, and cleaned the paint from between his sharp toes. I finished the walls, windowsills, and bedspreads, which now appeared as a light shade of pink. Finally, I sat down to examine my painting.

There were three crimson paw prints spaciously arranged across the page. They just missed the face of my daughter. They also missed Chuck's own painted image, glaring up at me defiantly. The alizarin crimson held true to its nature, stubbornly refusing any efforts to remove it.

I decided I was left with two options. Either I could throw away my painting and begin again, or I could change my plans and work around the stains. The challenge of finding a way to ignore the crimson paw prints and paint in the delicate white sundresses was what I needed on this day that the Lord had made.

As I painted, I began to relax. My mind settled, then cleared. I studied my composition and thought about changes. The darker background of green and blue bushes might camouflage the path of paw prints.

As I painted, the crimson stains began to disappear. I also noticed, much to my surprise, that the deep rich background color accentuated the feeling of sunshine and warmth in the foreground. The darkness made the tea party glow in comparison. Changing the painting actually improved it. Lucky for Chuck!

When God created this perfect world, he knew it would become tainted with sin. He sent his Son, Jesus, to wash clean the sins of the world with his own crimson blood. Now "he does not treat us as our sins deserve or repay us according to our iniquities. For as high as the heavens are above the earth, so great is his love for those who fear him; as far as the east is from the west, so far has he removed our transgressions from us" (Psalm 103:10-12).

The more I realize what God has done for me, the more it affects my life. He established a perfect plan just for me. I, on the other hand, have muddled up his plans with sin. But instead of tossing me aside, God decided to redeem the work begun in me.

God's redemptive work goes beyond my capacity to reason. Why would a holy God want to die for someone who stains her life daily with willful disobedience?

Ah! That's the real beauty of it all. My Savior showers his love on me in the form of never-ending, unlimited, no-strings-attached forgiveness. The power of his forgiveness opens up endless possibilities.

And then . . . peace

I catch myself lost in thought as I enjoy a cup of coffee while sitting in my quiet living room. The house is cool, and I am thankful for the warmth of my sweater. The rest of the family will be up soon. But right now it is peaceful. The only sound is the contented purring next to me. In this stillness it is easy to contemplate God. His words settle in my heart. "If I rise on the wings of the dawn, if I settle on the far side of the sea, even there your hand will guide me, your right hand will hold me fast" (Psalm 139). The peace of the moment penetrates deep into my soul.

It always amazes me how I feel fresh and new as I read these ancient words. I guess it shouldn't surprise me. God speaks unchanging words. He allows the eyes of my heart to be enlightened.

I finish my cup of coffee but do not get up. There is great satisfaction in this peaceful reminiscing; I count my blessings and measure the wealth of my answered prayers. I think of our children—the blessings I thought I would never possess. Katherine, with her long, wavy brown hair, who still talks through her moments. Elizabeth, with such big eyes as a toddler, soaking up any information that passed her way. And Dan, our firstborn, who enjoys the explorations of learning and savors the language of music. He nears that time in his life when he will choose his own paths.

Jesus said, "Everyone who hears these words of mine and puts them into practice is like a wise man who built his house on the rock" (Matthew 7:24). As I see the Lord guiding the lives of our children and feel the undeserved windfall of his blessings, the wisdom of putting the Savior's words into practice in our home just seems so practical. Building on Jesus' words is the common sense of faith.

Holding hands

I am enjoying my contented rest. Perhaps I need to contemplate my blessings more often—to take time and be still. My husband joins me for his second cup of coffee. He glances my way and offers me more. After filling my cup, he sits down and holds my hand, a continuation of the evening before.

We celebrated our anniversary with a *Sunset Special* at a local restaurant. Sitting at a small, round table for two, we watched the afternoon settle. The glittering sunshine reflected on the harbor below the restaurant. A slight breeze filled the sails of the boats still full of life on the Sound. The sky was summer blue, stretching past the Olympic Mountains in the distance. We held hands, enjoying our quiet companionship. As the evening sky began to color the landscape, we shared a wonderful meal.

Afterwards we enjoyed a walk along the waterfront. The breeze changed direction, bringing an offshore evening coolness. We watched as new, darker, richer, warmer colors appeared in the sky, stretching into a magnificent sunset.

Holding Mark's hand warmed me inside. We talked about the first time we had held hands, walking along the shores of Lake Michigan. Again, the overwhelming volume of my blessings filled me with awe. "How precious to me are your thoughts, O God! How vast is the sum of them!" (Psalm 139:17). God has blessed me beyond all measure. His promises are true. The challenge is in knowing what to do with them all.

What a challenge! The Lord himself says, "See if I will not throw open the floodgates of heaven and pour out so much blessing that you will not have room enough for it" (Malachi 3:10). His floodgates are open. I am rich beyond the limits of my own imagination.

Shasta, the purring calico, stretches next to me, expecting some attention. She is a beautiful conglomeration of mismatched colors. It would be interesting to put her in a painting.

I think again about Chuck. He was a cool cat. He let the kids in the neighborhood dress him up. He went for rides in wagons filled with blankets. And he always came running, purring when I called. So, I forgave him the paint incident. But I regret that I forgot to take a photo of the finished work for my records. I entered the painting in a local show where it sold the first day. When I delivered the painting, I shared Chuck's story. It delighted the new owner of the watercolor. Chuck now glares defiantly in her kitchen, as my daughters continue to pour that refreshing lemonade.

I give Shasta the attention she is seeking. She rubs against me, declaring that she owns me for the moment. She would not have liked Chuck.

Our treasures begin waking up. They appear in the living room one by one, disheveled from their sleep. We will share a warm breakfast together, followed by our morning devotion. Then we'll start the day with prayer, asking for new opportunities. When we leave the table, we will go in different directions. The Lord will guide each of us on a different path, but holding us all in his right hand.

I don't want to let go of the comfort of this moment. How much better to secure it close to my heart so that I can revisit it again and again, like a cherished photograph! My heart whispers again, "This is the day the LORD has made."

There will be many more. Like the soaring heights of our mountains these days remind me of our limitless God. "From everlasting to everlasting the LORD's love is with those who fear him, and his righteousness with their children's children—with those who keep his covenant and remember to obey his precepts" (Psalm 103:17,18).

God's Word wraps around me and holds me close, like my comfortable, old sweater. As I get out the ingredients for fresh waffles, I silently say a prayer of thanks. The Lord has literally poured his blessings into my life by the handful, with hands that still show where nails tore through flesh. I praise him for the great things he has done. It is a moment to rejoice. Let this new day begin!